Bounce Forward

Bounce Forward

The Extraordinary Resilience of Nurse Leadership

Elle Allison-Napolitano, PhD
Daniel J. Pesut, PhD, RN, PMHCNS-BC, FAAN

American Nurses Association
Silver Spring, Maryland • 2015

AMERICAN NURSES
ASSOCIATION

American Nurses Association
8515 Georgia Avenue, Suite 400
Silver Spring, MD 20910-3492
1-800-274-4ANA
www.NursingWorld.org

Published by Nursesbooks.org
The Publishing Program of ANA
www.Nursesbooks.org/

The American Nurses Association (ANA) is the only full-service professional organization representing the interests of the nation's 3.1 million
registered nurses through its constituent/state nurses associations and
its organizational affiliates. The ANA advances the nursing profession
by fostering high standards of nursing practice, promoting the rights of
nurses in the workplace, projecting a positive and realistic view of nursing,
and by lobbying the Congress and regulatory agencies on healthcare issues
affecting nurses and the public.

Cataloging-in-Publication Data is available from the Library of Congress.

978-1-55810-591-1
First printing: March 2015

SAN: 851-3481   3/2015

In the spirit of renewal, this book is dedicated to past, present and next generation nursing leaders

Contents

Acknowledgments

The following nurse leaders participated in individual interviews with Elle Allison-Napolitano throughout 2014:

Dean Bern Melnyk, PhD, RN, CPNP/PMHNP, FAANP, FNAP, FAAN

Leslie S. Parran, MS, RN, AOCN, NE-BC, BMTCN

Rachelle Larsen, PhD, RN,

Megan Daman, MA, RN, ACNS-BC

Stephanie Youngberg, BS, RN

Lisa McDonald, RN, BSN, CRNFA

Connie Hill, PhD, RN

Donea Shane, PhD, Former Dean, School of Nursing, University of New Mexico

Marcia McCormick, MA, BSN, RN

Pat Murphy MSE, LP, LICSW, RN

Sharon Rorhbach, RN, Founder of Nurses for Newborns

Debbie Layton, RN

The following nurses leaders, who are all in the DNP program at San Francisco University, participated in a focus group with Elle Allison-Napolitano in San Francisco on April 7, 2014:

Tarina Kwong, MSN, RN

Richard Billingsley, MHA, MSN, RN

Sandra Gregg, MHA, MS, RN

Lisa Price, MPA, RN, Oakland, CA

Katherine Bullard, DNP, RN, Texas

Marjorie Barter, EdD, RN, CNL, CENP

Anne Naidoo, DNPc, RN, CPHHA, Riyodh, Saudi Arabia

Tanya Osborne-McKenzie, DNP, MSN, MBVA, RN, Salinas, CA

Katherine Edrington, DNP, RN, Loveland, OH

Nan Ybarra, MBA, BSN, RN, NEA-BC

The following nurse leaders participated in a focus group held at San Francisco University with Elle Allison-Napolitano and Dan Pesut on June 13, 2014:

Juli Maxworthy, DNP, MSN, MBA, RN, CNL, CPHQ, CPPS, CHSE, University of San Francisco, CA

Margaret Hansen, EdD, MSN, RN

Sara Guido, DNP, RN, BC-NE

Cathy Coleman, DNP, MSN, RN, OCN, CPHQ, CNL

Ebin Howard, PhD, MBA, RN

Enna Trevathan, DNP, MSN, MBA, RN, CNL

Shannon Nell, DNP, MBA, BCur, RN, Director of Nursing and Nursing Education, Sandton, South Africa

Mary Lou DeNatale, EdD, RN, CNL

Judith Karshmer, PhD, PMHCNS-BC

The art on pages 3, 35, 57, and 83 were created by Becky Wagley of Wagley Creative of Santa Rosa Beach, Florida.

About the Authors

Elle Allison-Napolitano, PhD—Back in 2006, she published her dissertation on the nature of wisdom in nurses. What she found was so astounding and yet so practical, that she decided to devote her life's work to developing tools, processes and perspectives that help more people, teams and whole organizations operate from the position of wisdom. As founder and president of Wisdom Out, Elle works with leaders, aspiring leaders, senior leadership teams, work teams and leadership coaches, to teach them the strategies, practices, and tools they need to increase their organization's capacity for positive change and sustainable results.

Elle is author of several books and articles on transformational leadership, focusing on wisdom, resilience, renewal, and strategies for leadership sustainability. An educator, speaker, consultant, leadership coach, he earned her PhD in Organizational Learning from the University of New Mexico and is a graduate of the National Staff Development. She offers customized workshops, leadership academies and keynotes—all of which she intertwines with stories of real leaders who face change and adversity with pluck, grace, and a wicked sense of humor that brings them a sense of renewal and joy.

Daniel J. Pesut, PhD, RN, PMHCNS-BC, FAAN—Dan is Professor of Nursing in the Nursing Population Health and Systems Cooperative Unit of the School of Nursing at the University of Minnesota, and Director of the Katharine J. Densford International Center for Nursing Leadership. He holds the Katherine R. and C. Walton Lillehei Chair in Nursing Leadership. Dan earned a PhD in Nursing from the University of Michigan, a Master's Degree in Psychiatric Mental Health Nursing from the University of Texas Health Science Center in

San Antonio, TX and BS degree in Nursing from Northern Illinois University, DeKalb, IL. He is internationally known for his work in nursing education and creative-teaching learning methods, clinical reasoning, futures thinking, and leadership development in the health professions.

Dan has completed Certificates in Management Development from Harvard Institute for Higher Education; Core Mediation Skills Training from the International Association of Dispute Resolution (IARD); and a certificate in Integral Studies from Fielding Graduate University. He is past President (2003–2005) of the Honor Society of Nursing, Sigma Theta Tau International, and a Fellow in the American Academy of Nursing. He is also a certified Hudson Institute coach. He is the recipient of numerous awards including an Army Commendation Award while on active duty (1975–1978) in the U.S. Army Nurse Corps; the Honor Society of Nursing, Sigma Theta Tau International Edith Moore Copeland Founder's Award for Excellence in Creativity; The American Assembly for Men in Nursing Luther Christman Award.

His most creative contributions to the world, in partnership with his wife Susan Ziel, are his culturally creative children, Elliott and Erin.

Preface

Every book like this one begins with a purpose, a reason that usually has to do with a desire to improve conditions and situations, to help people solve vexing problems, and to present information organized in a manner that creates inspiration and encourages the heart. In addition to being nurse champions and in Dan's case, a nurse leader long interested in creating healthy work environments characterized by renewal, we also came to write this book as a way to support nurse leaders as they strive every day to reach the vision of the future of nursing, presented in the 2010 Institute of Medicine (IOM) report (*The Future of Nursing: Leading Change, Advancing Health*).

This particular book focuses on leadership resilience in the profession of nursing, where powerful forces of change have made for an exceptionally demanding landscape. Many of the changes effecting nursing practice are focused on improving patient care, efficiency, and quality of service. These changes are important and are challenging. They require new ways of thinking and leading and they require an extraordinary form of resilience, one that does more than restore the status quo, but actually inspires action in new realities.

The drivers of these changes in nursing are many, including the spiraling cost of health care, and a real or perceived sense that healthcare costs exceed the value produced. Other drivers include increased public awareness and involvement in their health care and an increase in coincident disease leading to complexities in patient care. In addition, new technologies—though often ultimately helpful—take time to learn and implement. The profession also continues to face a dire and growing shortage of nurses and qualified nurse educators capable of critical thinking, evidence-based practice, strong leadership, professionalism, and innovation (Institute of Medicine, 2010; American Nurses Association, 2013).

An earlier IOM report, *Crossing the Quality Chasm* (2001), offered a landmark study calling for members of the nursing profession to create and develop new models of leadership that would transform and positively influence the future direction of healthcare delivery in the United States. Specifically, the IOM suggested nurse leaders needed to exert influence to redesign care delivery models, champion the use of clinical information systems and evidence-based practice, and support patient learning in service of health and healthy lifestyles.

The type of transformational change described in both the 2001 and the 2010 IOM reports require leadership resilience. One of the major purposes of this book therefore, is to provide nurses in practice, education, and community contexts a model and methods to cultivate the personal, professional, and organizational resilience necessary to achieve the vision of a transformed 21st century healthcare system. While there are a number of national leadership competencies and standards that exist (National Healthcare Leadership Competency and ANA Leadership Institute Competency Model, 2013), we believe that nurse leaders also benefit from the wisdom gleaned from practitioners in the field.

We also have personal reasons for writing this book, stemming from lifelong commitments to nurses and to the profession. Elle Allison-Napolitano is a nurse champion who has investigated the wisdom of nurses in practice, education, and research contexts. Through her research and work in organizational learning, she has created and continues to evolve a model of leadership resilience that contributes to personal and professional renewal through attention to things that matter. Elle is invested in helping people in all fields to acquire the knowledge, skills, and abilities to bounce forward in the face of change and leadership challenges. She wrote the first version of this book (Allison-Napolitano, 2014) for school system educators who, similar to nurses, are called upon to move complex organizations into an ambiguous future. Her desire to bring a similar resource to nurse leaders led her to invite Dan to collaborate with her on this version for nurses.

Daniel Pesut is a nurse educator who has spent 39 years helping people develop the critical and creative mindset that supports the development of leadership insights. He has a long-standing interest in supporting the personal and professional renewal of nurses in practice, education, and research contexts

(Pesut, 2001; 2007; 2008; 2012). When he was president of the Honor Society of Nursing, Sigma Theta Tau International (2003–2005), his call to action was: Create the Future through Renewal. Dan became aware of Elle's wisdom and work with nurses while he was president and has continued to follow the development and evolution of her ideas and research. Partnering with Elle in the creation of this book about nurse leadership resilience is a great opportunity.

Together we hope the stories, models, and methods we share with you will influence your thinking, being, and doing as you continue to contribute your nursing leadership influence to the desired 21st century healthcare system of the future.

Introduction

A Book About Leadership Resilience

To my extreme mortification I grow wiser every day.

—Lady Mary Wortley Montagu

Amy Smith is a charge nurse of ambulatory surgery at a university health system serving a large northwest region of the United States. Over the last four decades, the community's ethnic diversity has increased drastically, becoming home to large populations of immigrants from all over the world. Languages spoken in the region include Spanish and Hmong, over 30 African languages, Vietnamese, Chinese, French, Russian, and Laotian. Amy, who has been charge nurse for three years, enjoys guiding the nurses she supervises and is known for assuring that nurses receive the training they need to stay current and to provide relevant care.

Over the last year, Amy introduced stand up meetings called huddles to the nursing teams, as a way to encourage daily focus on communication about patients. As a champion for the huddle initiative, Amy believed the huddles improved relationships between nurses and staff and therefore had a positive effect on patient care. In the last month, residents and a few other health-care employees began to observe the huddle in order to get updates for the day. Amy was pretty happy with how the huddles were going but some of the residents and other observers had a habit of interrupting the conversation to interject their ideas and opinions. Recently she was thinking that the observers could benefit from specific training on the process and the overall purpose of huddles. She intended to approach the supervising physician about this the following week.

Then it happened. Amy was called to a late Friday afternoon meeting with Terry, the senior nurse manager to review some red flags in patient quality and satisfaction data. At the meeting, Terry told Amy that over the past three months patient satisfaction has steadily decreased in ambulatory surgery. "This isn't a fluke," she told Amy. "It really is a trend." As a side note, Terry also told Amy that she had received a complaint from a nurse, saying that certain people dominated the stand-up huddles and that these individuals intimidated many of the nurses. "Amy, haven't you noticed that more and more nurses speak less and less in the huddle?" Terry added, "I know you aspire to become a nurse manager in the hospital someday, but Amy, between the decline in patient satisfaction and complaints from the nursing staff, I'm afraid you may be putting your career goals in jeopardy."

Amy's story is not unique. Nurse leaders function in hospitals and healthcare facilities; complex organizations, ripe for conflict, confusion, and miscommunication. When changing external forces and the need for rapid response are added to this already complex mix, nurse leaders like Amy frequently find themselves presented with challenges that become defining moments in their career. Depending on her capacity for leadership resilience, Amy could respond to the set of challenges before her with the grace and pluck characteristic of leadership resilience. Or, achieving a middle ground, Amy could seek to restore the status quo, neither crashing and burning but also not gaining forward motion from the experience. Most devastating, she could descend into non-resilience. The question therefore is not about how well Amy will prevent adversities like this one from occurring, but about how she will respond and transform this particular challenge into growth.

Responding to Adversity: A Hallmark of Wisdom

The genesis of this book goes back to the year 2000, when, as part of my doctoral dissertation research, I (Elle) investigated the nature of wisdom in nurses who were nominated by peers who thought them to be wise. Through the qualitative research process known as the long interview, I gathered the rich and detailed stories of the nurses who agreed to participate in my study. And what stories they had to tell!

As I began to analyze and code the details of these interviews, several patterns began to emerge. First, many stories began with an event that represented a tremendous loss or adversity. I wasn't surprised about this finding—after all, adversity is neither rare nor unusual and who among us hasn't experienced loss? What was more compelling about the stories these wise nurses told, however, was that they consistently included redemptive sequences where new perspectives allowed them to create something good out of the adversities they faced (Tedeschi & Calhoun, 1995; Lauritzen & Jaegar, 1997; and Turner & Cox, 2004). Consistent with Mezirow's assertion that a "new way of seeing has to lead to some kind of action," these wise nurses demonstrated a knack for transforming adversity into energy to create something better—a program, a culture, or a new process that served a greater good for patients, colleagues, their organizations, and the field of health care (2000, p. 335). Wise nurses seem to possess an incredible bias for action and for being willing to create evidence behind their innovative ideas.

Arriving at something good out of something bad gave meaning to the losses and adversities these nurses encountered in life and work. For many, the redemptive sequence was the capstone of a transformational learning process that led many of these wise nurses to discover what they believe is their true purpose on earth and in their role in health care. At a time when studies show that as many as 15% of nurses are disengaged from working toward the mission of their organizations (Gallup, 2013, p. 33), the fact that adversity can lead to meaning and purpose highlights the importance of leadership resilience

About This Book: An Extraordinary Form of Resilience

This is a book about an extraordinary form of resilience that we call "leadership resilience." We define leadership resilience as the experience of growing stronger in the face of adversity, and helping oneself and others to transform the negative experience into energy. This energy is then used to create new realities and possibilities not just for achieving goals, but to play a bigger game, creating organizational outcomes that serve a greater good. The book is an invitation for you to reflect and gain insights into the important difference between ordinary resilience and leadership resilience. It achieves this goal by presenting a model and a set of strategies derived from real-life stories and insights gained from experienced nurse leaders who have embodied and modeled leadership resilience during times of challenge and disruptive change.

As opposed to bouncing back, a colloquialism that represents ordinary resilience, leadership resilience is characterized by bouncing forward, by the achievement of a new and more complex equilibrium that signifies personal, professional, and organizational learning. Most leadership training and development programs do not help leaders learn what it means to practice the extraordinary resilience they need to lead in the face of adversity. Without leadership resilience insights, many nurse leaders believe they lack something vital that enables them to love their work and appreciate the meaning in how they act and what they do.

The goal of this book, therefore, is to close the gap between the complex demands organizations make of nurse leaders and the personal and professional resilience tools they need to master in order to meet those demands.

The Gifts of Leadership Resilience

Wise nurses have much to teach us about leadership resilience. Wise nurses faced everything that came their way with uncanny optimism and used adversity to propel themselves forward. They didn't just bounce back from adversity; they bounced forward.

One of the most helpful insights gleaned from the nurses in my (Elle's) initial study is realizing that wisdom is not synonymous with perfection. The poignant lesson this insight provides for nurse leaders in complex organizations is that adversity is neither rare nor unusual and even wise nurse leaders do not possess a magic bullet for staving off loss, disappointment, and sorrow. In fact, since unfortunate things happen to everyone, whether we have our ducks in a row and all our i's dotted and t's crossed or not, our energy is far better placed in transforming inevitable loss into opportunity. How to do this is the subject of this book, and more specifically, how to do it as a *leader*, when everyone is watching you, and either depending on you or daring you to take the first step.

Learning Resilience

Writing about what we think of as ordinary resilience, the American Psychological Association (APA) offers this observation: "Resilience is not a trait that people either have or do not have. It involves behaviors, thoughts and actions that can be learned and developed by anyone" (APA, 2002). Given the fact that the adversities that befall nurse leaders are neither unusual nor uncommon, whatever your current capacity for resilience, you can and will become even more resilient.

If there is anything daunting about growing in leadership resilience, it's that you can't just read about it or hear about it and expect to become more resilient, any more than you can watch the cooking channel on TV and then go into the kitchen expecting to find the same meal waiting for you at the table. Becoming more resilient comes down to your determination to change existing habits and learn new ways of being and leading in the face of adversity. Resilience may be hard won, but leaders who choose to build their personal resilience, and create resilient organizations, will understand the truth of what Friedrich Nietzsche meant when he said, "That which does not kill us makes us stronger."

Orientation to This Book

This book introduces leadership resilience. Therefore, this book does not attempt to present the many and varied theories of ordinary resilience. In fact, we propose that leadership requires an extraordinary form of resilience that goes far beyond the characteristics of ordinary resilience. In addition, this book does not seek to cover the entire territory of leadership during times of change, but it does focus on the extra requirements of leadership resilience during disruptive change.

To accomplish this focus, we've delved into relevant information known about resilience and applied it to leadership. The literature on which we have relied is not inclusive, but is representative of several fields of study including wisdom, post-traumatic growth, positive psychology, transformational leadership, emotional intelligence, organizational learning, neuroscience, behavioral economics, and adaptive change theory.

Because of my (Elle's) long tradition of using stories and observations of real people navigating the challenges and opportunities of their lives and work, the ideas and tools you'll find in this book are bolstered with stories from interviews and focus groups with real nurse leaders facing adversity in their work. It is only through the job-embedded stories of what happens, and what leaders do in response to what happens that we see resilience in action. Stories make resilience visible.

An Inside-out Approach

Gandhi's words, "Be the change you want to see in the world," have engendered transformational leadership in individuals from all walks of life and livelihood. When it comes to leadership resilience, Gandhi's words are iron-clad, for leaders are only as resilient in their work as they are personally, and resilient organizations depend on resilient leadership. For these reasons, this book begins at the personal level and then scales to the organization. All of the ideas about leadership resilience offered to you in this book are actionable. You can begin to practice them immediately, and over time you'll become more resilient and will inspire resilience in others.

Book Organization

In the chapters that follow, you will find a model that illuminates the concept of leadership resilience, what it takes to become a resilient leader, how to put your leadership resilience into action, and how to foster resilient organizations.

Following this Introduction, **Part I** of this book contains two chapters:

- **Chapter 1** presents three different scenarios about Amy, the nurse leader you read about at the beginning of this introduction. The case study scenarios illustrate how leadership resilience differs from ordinary resilience, and reveal its transformational qualities and nature. You will also recognize the types of adversities that you or nurse colleagues may have experienced that call for resilient leadership responses.

- **Chapter 2** introduces the Wisdom Out Leadership Resilience Model, which is composed of three parts: (1) The enabling capacities of leadership (relationships, resonance, and renewal); (2) Six principles that activate Leadership Resilience in Action (stay calm; carry on; accept the new reality; want something more; instigate adaptive action; reflect, celebrate, and renew); (3) Attention to the ecosystem of the larger organization in which resilient leadership thrives.

Part II contains three chapters, each of which focuses on one of the three leadership resilience-enabling capacities. The enabling capacities make leadership resilience possible. Each chapter offers you the opportunity to complete an inventory that allows you to reflect on your current levels with regard to each enabling capacity and provide a springboard for conversation. Each chapter also contains approaches for bringing the resilience-enabling capacities to life in complex organizational contexts.

- **Chapter 3** focuses on the importance of the enabling capacity of renewal, which is the source of energy for sustaining leadership resilience. This chapter presents research about what people find energizing during the workday and it encourages you to implement on the job strategies for renewal.

- **Chapter 4** illuminates the enabling capacity of resonance—the ability of a leader to ignite the organization with emotions that help them bounce forward and take action in the aftermath of change. The chapter provides strategies and techniques to cultivate resonance with others.

- **Chapter 5** delves into the enabling capacity of relationships—those personal and professional networks that provide support during times of adversity. The chapter highlights characteristics of non-resilience in self and others and prompts you to be vigilant about non-resilient individuals that may hinder or impede the development of resilience.

Part III takes us to the second part of the Wisdom Out Leadership Resilience Model, which focuses on Leadership Resilience in Action. Part III consists of six chapters. Like the chapters before them, they offer specific strategies and tools. This section describes and explains six essential resilient leadership actions:

- **Chapter 6.** Stay Calm
- **Chapter 7.** Carry On
- **Chapter 8.** Accept the New Reality
- **Chapter 9.** Want Something More
- **Chapter 10.** Instigate Adaptive Action
- **Chapter 11.** Reflect, Celebrate, and Renew

Part IV Synthesizing the New Resilience: Assessing Your Organization's Level of Risk for Non-Resilience scales resilience to teams and organizations and presents an organizational Resilience Risk Assessment that leaders can use to introduce helpful disruption, conversations, and learning dialogues with the intention of stimulating and challenging leaders in an organization to deal proactively with vulnerabilities that may undermine the organization or systems in which people operate.

- **Afterword.** Forgive Yourself Every Day, closes out the book with a reminder that, in terms of sustaining your practice of leadership resilience, the strategy that overarches all the other, forgiving yourself everyday frees you to bounce forward and continue your work for a greater good.

Special Features and Suggestions

Although you certainly may read this book on your own and hopefully gain much from it, leadership resilience is a quality acquired by taking risks that test your mettle on the job. For that reason, we invite you to read the book with colleagues, your management leadership team, protégés, or with mentors and coaches. To empower you toward this end, every chapter contains "Activities and Questions," which stimulate ideas and actions about leadership resilience. You can use these activities and questions to get your own resilience juices flowing or to coach another person or team to do the same.

Once you begin work on your personal leadership resilience and on the leadership resilience of the teams you lead, you will increase your capacity to influence others on a larger scale within your own organization and within the greater profession of nursing.

The other special features you'll find in this book include

- Stories, reflections, and ideas from effective nurse leaders who love their work, achieve results, and make a difference.
- Inventories you can take in the book or online.
- Strategies, tools, and helpful sidebars.
- A resilience risk assessment to use with your teams and colleagues to evaluate your organization for vulnerabilities in resilience.
- An appendix, with a short list of movies, music, literature, and poems that conjure up ideas of leadership resilience (if you want to contribute to this list, you can find the blog at www.wisdomout.com).
- Links to leadership resources like the Honor Society of Nursing Sigma Theta Tau International Leadership Institute at http://www.nursingsociety.org/LeadershipInstitute/
- Links to the American Nurses Association Leadership Institute at http://www.ana-leadershipinstitute.org/

Follow-Up

The reason this book is filled with rich stories of tribulations and triumph is because we all have them. Stories really are the only way we see leadership resilience. In this spirit, you are invited to continue your journey toward leadership resilience by participating in additional professional development opportunities:

- If you have a resilience story you want to share, or if you try out some of the ideas in this book and you want to share your insights, either e-mail Elle at elle@wisdomout.com or call her at 925-786-0987.
- Visit www.WisdomOut.com and sign up for the newsletter, view videos, read articles, and sign up for complimentary webinars focusing on the ideas in this book.
- Talk with Elle about providing your organization with keynotes, workshops, and boot camps. Or set up a series of webinars to correspond to the chapters your leadership team or your leadership resilience study group is most curious about.
- Visit the ANA website at http://www.nursingworld.org and other nurse leaders' organizations for additional support in your leadership journey. The ANA provides numerous opportunities for emerging and developing leaders as well as for advanced leaders to learn.
- Visit the website for the Katharine J. Densford International Center for Nursing at http://www.nursing.umn.edu/densford/ to participate in ongoing professional development, listen and watch recorded interviews with famous nurse leaders, and read Dan's Meta Reflection Blog on various issues in nursing and nurse education, practice, and research.

Five Good Reasons to Increase Your Leadership Resilience

1. Even with your ducks in a row, anything can happen unexpectedly. Rather than rail against adversity, better to learn resilience.

2. You can. Resilience is not something you either have or do not have; you can learn to become more resilient.

3. Resilient leaders achieve more goals.

4. Resilient leaders manage the stress of change better than leaders who are not resilient.

5. The same characteristics inherent to leadership resilience also make life better.

1

A New Resilience for a New Type of Nurse Leader

1

Bounce Forward

Apparently, anything can happen today.

—Mark Twain

Return for a moment to Amy, the nurse you met in the Introduction to this book. Now, let's imagine three different responses—leadership resilience, ordinary resilience, and then non-resilience—that Amy could have to this disruptive and unexpected adversity. It seems that the best way to reveal the similarities and differences between each is to begin with considering a response characterized by leadership resilience—a response that transcends the ordinary to achieve something different, something more. Then we'll look at how Amy could respond with ordinary resilience. Finally, providing sharp contrast to both, we'll look at a completely non-resilient response.

Amy Responds with Leadership Resilience

Amy sat for several minutes in the quiet of her office to absorb the details of the situation and all of its implications. She pulled up the patient satisfaction data on her computer and began to pore over the details. When she disaggregated the data by cultural groups, she saw that patients from the growing African populations were less satisfied with their experience in ambulatory surgery than other groups of community members. *Well, this is interesting and makes perfect sense*, Amy thought as she packed up her briefcase to go home. *Our community demographics have changed over the last two years, yet we have not focused on understanding their unique needs.* Amy realized that she had failed to review the feedback forms often enough or with the attention to detail she knows she should. Amy thought, *From now on, I need to involve the team in looking at the disaggregated data. The more specific we are about patient needs, the better we can meet them.*

On her way out to the parking lot, Amy stopped at the desk of her administrative assistant to go over the calendar for the coming week. When they finished, she wished him a good weekend and drove to the market to pick up the chicken she wanted to cook for her husband's birthday barbeque on Saturday. While waiting in line at the grocery store, she sent a text to Ron, an old friend of hers. Though now retired from managing a large non-profit organization, Ron had broad leadership experience and was fond of Amy and always eager to mentor her. Amy arranged to meet him for coffee on Sunday afternoon.

On Saturday, as she enjoyed her husband's birthday celebration, Amy's mind and heart played around with the dilemma before her. She watched her three-year-old grandson, who had just learned to walk, intrepidly approach and remove everything between himself and the things he wanted—cookies on the counter top, pots and pans in the cabinets, the dog. She kept thinking, *Where there is a will there is always a way. It just might not be MY preferred way!*

Over the next two months, here are the specific actions Amy took:

- She met with her friend Ron. When Amy told Ron about her meeting with Terry, Amy was a bit surprised that Ron focused on the huddles just as much as he did the low patient satisfaction scores. When he asked Amy to describe the purpose of the huddles, Amy talked about how they help nursing teams focus on specific aspects of patient care. In the process of giving Ron the details, she had what felt like a sudden insight. "Aha," she told Ron. "With proper execution, the huddles could be a vehicle for daily focus on patient satisfaction!"

- Amy met with her nurses to tell them a challenge came up in patient satisfaction data. She asked what she could do for them in the short run to support them.

- Amy met with the education team and put together a program to formally teach the huddle process to the teams, including the interns who were interested in participating. They made patient satisfaction the focus of the huddle.

- After the education team provided training on the huddles, Amy asked for a team huddle coach to help them fully implement the practice and to sustain the procedure and the norms.

- One nurse, who was Somali, introduced a cultural care checklist for nurses to use with patients regarding their care and received permission to try it out. A few other nurses volunteered to try it out too.

- After several weeks, patient satisfaction data began to increase. The teams continued to focus the huddles on patient satisfaction and they began to think of other factors to address.

- The team of nurses who had beta tested the cultural care checklist revised and honed it further and did several mini in-service trainings to introduce it to the rest of the team.

- As the team began to experience positive results both with the huddle and with patient satisfaction data, the nurse education team asked if they could make a training video showcasing their practice.

- Amy's son taught her how to record verbal e-mail messages on her cell phone. After a few false starts, she began sending 30-second messages acknowledging one or two different nurses at the end of each day.

- Amy invited the nurses to prepare a poster presentation for the next in-hospital conference, showcasing the link between focused huddles and improvements in patient satisfaction outcomes.

Within Amy's leadership resilience response, we see she took steps to transform this particular challenge into an advantage—the silk purse from the sow's ear, so to speak. Amy's knack for achieving positive change in response to adversity characterizes leadership resilience and differentiates it from ordinary resilience and certainly from non-resilience. The next section describes a response more typical of ordinary resilience. As you read it, begin to notice the differences between ordinary resilience and leadership resilience.

Amy Responds with Ordinary Resilience

After meeting with Terry, Amy barely remembered walking back to her office area. She felt like someone had pulled a rug out from underneath her feet and she was falling in slow motion. Amy sat at her desk, her hands shaking as she pulled up the patient satisfaction data on her computer so she could pore over it in detail. When she disaggregated the data by cultural groups, she saw that patients from the growing African population were less satisfied with their experience in ambulatory surgery than other groups of community members. She realized that she had failed to review the feedback forms often enough or with the attention to detail she knows she should. Amy thought, *From now on, I will look at customer satisfaction data at the end of every single day.*

Amy's mind then turned to the matter of the huddles. Although an entirely different issue, maybe the huddles were distracting her from other responsibilities—such as examining patient satisfaction data in detail—and therefore were part of the problem. *The huddles are not worth doing if the patients are not satisfied with the experience they have here with us,* she thought.

Glancing at the clock Amy saw that it was already late in the day and she still had to stop at the market to buy chicken for her husband's birthday barbeque on Saturday. After she packed up her briefcase, she sent an email to the nursing staff to let them know that patient satisfaction had dropped significantly and therefore the huddles were canceled for now. She wrote, "I encourage you all to give your full attention to assuring that every patient has the best experience possible here at our ambulatory surgical center."

Amy then drove to the market to pick up the chicken she wanted to cook for the barbeque. Over the weekend, Amy had some difficulty sleeping and felt removed from her husband and the joy of his birthday. *How can I get my department and my career back on track?*

Ultimately, here are some of the decisions Amy made and actions she took as she responded to this situation:

- She put the huddles on hold, telling the nurses that she wanted to first concentrate on the decrease in patient satisfaction. She promised she would provide training before they reinstated the huddle practice.
- She put together a task force to examine patient satisfaction data, focusing specifically on information from the growing African patient population and other diverse ethnic sub-groups.
- She increased her interactions with patients from various ethnic subgroups and noted her observations and ideas for improving cultural sensitivity and care.

- She arranged for staff to participate in a cultural care inventory in order to self-assess and set goals to increase competency
- She made several online and in-person workshops available to staff, as well as training opportunities on how to increase personal cultural competency.
- She hoped that the focus on cultural care for patients would create better relationships between staff members as well.

When we imagine Amy responding with ordinary resilience, we see that she seeks to restore her department and her career to previous levels of functioning and possibility. Ordinary resilience in other words, creates outcomes that resemble the current status quo, which is why people commonly refer to it as the ability to bounce back. Certainly, ordinary resilience is not a bad response—bouncing back is a good thing. But ordinary resilience lacks the transformational aspect of leadership resilience. Bouncing back is not the same thing as moving forward.

The next section describes a non-resilient response to the same situation. As you read Amy's hypothetical non-resilient response, notice and infer the lacking personal characteristics and capacities and the effect they have on Amy as she responds.

Amy Responds with Non-Resilience

After meeting with Terry, Amy was in disbelief. How could Terry attack her this way? She hurried to the hospital parking lot and called Bill, a colleague in another department at the hospital who would listen to her complaints. "I'm so mad, I could spit," Amy told Bill. "You better watch your back too, Bill. Obviously upper management doesn't know the first thing about priorities around here."

When she finished her call to Bill, Amy trudged back to her office and slumped into her chair, completely defeated. She had taken her time and energy to institute huddles in order to improve things around here! She wondered who complained about being intimidated in the huddles and suspected it was Marge, a veteran nurse who never wanted to try anything new. Why did she even bother? And how dare Terry imply that Amy might not receive the promotion she so clearly deserved!

Amy's mind raced as she packed up her briefcase to go home. Without pausing, she turned to her computer and hammered out an email to everyone in her department. She wrote in the subject line: "Patients are not satisfied with our department." Then, she attached the data file and hit the "send" button.

Amy drove home, nearly forgetting to stop to buy the food she needed for her husband's birthday barbeque on Saturday. The kids would all be there, and she didn't think she would have the energy to deal with them and their needs, their stories, their idle chatter. Even the thought of seeing her baby grandson made her weary. "Maybe nothing really matters after all," she said out loud to her reflection in the rear view mirror. "Maybe my whole life has been one big, fat flop."

Amy's non-resilient response is enough to make you cringe. Although it is an exaggeration, you likely recognize the blunders that not only ruin careers but undermine patient and organizational outcomes.

By comparing and contrasting the similarities and differences between these three potential responses, we begin to understand what it means to be resilient and how leadership resilience goes beyond what we think of as ordinary resilience.

Ordinary Resilience

Before we leap into our exploration of leadership resilience, let's set the stage by first laying out what it means to have ordinary resilience, in other words, what it means to bounce back in the aftermath of adversity and disruptive change. The American Psychological Association (APA) captures the essence of resilience in this definition:

> Resilience is the process of adapting well in the face of adversity, trauma, tragedy, threats, or even significant sources of stress—such as family and relationship problems, serious health problems, or workplace and financial stressors. It means 'bouncing back' from difficult experiences. (APA, 2002)

Like the APA, many contemporary researchers of resilience highlight the role of adaptation in resilience and explore what it means to bounce back. A highly regarded researcher on bereavement and resilience, George Bonanno (2009) elaborates on the process of adapting well by describing resilient people as those who bounce back and continue forward in life with a sense of core purpose and meaning. Expanding the scope of resilience beyond individuals, researchers Zolli and Healy (2012) define resilience as "the capacity of a system, enterprise, or a person to maintain its core purpose and integrity in the face of dramatically changed circumstances" (p. 126). Writing about resilience in young people, Clay, Knibbs, and Joseph (2009) say resilience is "the ability to continue to function normally in spite of adversity" (p. 413), and Scales, Benson, Leffert, and Blyth (2000) describe it as the ability to overcome negative events and quickly return to pre-trauma levels of functioning.

Given the widely accepted definition of resilience as the ability to bounce back and carry on with life, what might seem amazing is the fact that most people are resilient even in the face of significant loss and challenge.

Beautifully Ordinary

In their book about why people, organizations, systems, and entire communities bounce back in the aftermath of hardship, Andrew Zolli and Ann Marie Healey (2012) relate early investigations in the field of psychological resilience and explain why we are often surprised to learn that most of us are, in fact, quite resilient. Zolli and Healy tell us that initially, resilience research focused on children who were survivors of the Nazi concentration camps or offspring of schizophrenic parents. Many of these children went on to live good and productive lives, in spite of their harsh experiences. Dominated by Freud's theory that grief is a lengthy and treacherous process, however, the social psychologists that studied these children believed they were witnessing "superkids" who were blessed with an unusual ability to cope. But one researcher, named Ann Masten, pointed out that while it certainly was amazing that these children thrived in the face of such hardship, it was not unusual that they did so. The reason, Masten said, is the presence of "basic human adaptational systems" that predispose all of us for bouncing back (Zolli & Healy, 2012, p. 122).

Resilience is Common

Again, according to the APA (2002), "Research has shown that resilience is ordinary, not extraordinary. People commonly demonstrate resilience. One example is the response of many Americans to the September 11, 2001, terrorist attacks and individuals' efforts to rebuild their lives." Martin Seligman, who is often called the father of positive psychology and leads a resilience training program for the United States military, says that how people respond to adversity is normally distributed, with the majority of people falling in the middle (2011b). In the middle are the resilient people—those who experienced a hardship but who bounced back physically and psychologically to where they were before the trauma. According to Seligman, on the lower end of the curve are the people who develop post-traumatic stress disorder (PTSD), and at the opposite end are those individuals who eventually experience post-traumatic growth.

George Bonanno's longitudinal studies on resilience after tragedies, such as natural disasters, the SARS epidemic, or even personal losses, reveal similar findings: Only about one-third of the population experiences PTSD while the rest either bounce back or show little effect to begin with. Post-traumatic growth experts Calhoun and Tedeschi (1995) are even more optimistic. They tell us that anywhere between 30% and up to 90% of the population actually experience growth eventually, as a result of facing serious trauma.

Interestingly, Zolli and Healy say the fact that the percentage of people who display resilience is greater than the percentage of people who display signs of PTSD, or other maladaptive responses to challenges, suggests that this natural design "ensures that there is always at least a sizable minority or even a majority, to take care of those deeply affected by trauma" (2012, p. 127).

What It Means to Be Resilient

Bouncing back is seen in what individuals do in the aftermath of disruptive change, particularly in the capacity they have to navigate toward resources that restore them after a setback (Zautra, Hall, & Murray, 2010). Resources might be physical, such as taking on a second job to mitigate a financial blow or installing rails in the bathroom to aid mobility after an illness. They could be social, such as establishing a new relationship or alliance with someone who can provide support, or they could be psychological, such as seeking out a therapist or learning how to reframe negative thoughts.

Being resilient does not mean that people do not feel distress, sadness, or anger. Even people who are ultimately strengthened by adversity may first traverse through a period of time looking decidedly non-resilient, perhaps feeling depressed, anxious, or even turning to drugs and alcohol. But in general, we see resilience in the capacity of people to navigate toward resources that allow them to absorb relatively high levels of disruptive change while exhibiting minimal unproductive behaviors that impede their ability to function.

The idea that resilience is seen in people who experience setbacks, but who cope and adjust so that they can return to their previous state of normal functioning, lends credence to the visual image of people bouncing back. The ability to bounce back from life's curve balls is what helps us make it through another day.

Factors That Mediate Ordinary Resilience

The factors that promote resilience are many and varied, providing count-less pathways for its development. A few prominent factors that appear in the literature include personality traits such as optimism and confidence (Bonanno, 2009; Bonanno, Galea, Bucciareli, & Vlahov, 2007; Seligman, 2011a), perceptions of control, feeling empowered to act, perceptions of the harm caused as a result of adversity and the extent to which it was intentional and permanent (Calhoun & Tedeschi, 2006), having self-agency to make plans and leverage resources in one's direction and delay immediate reward in order to achieve future goals (APA, 2002; Block & Block, 1980), the presence of strong social networks, mindfulness meditation and cognitive reframing, the ability to regulate emotions, thinking and believing that one has a meaningful purpose in life, that one can influence one's surroundings, and that negative experiences can indeed lead to learning and growth (Kobasa, 1979).

According to Zolli and Healy (2012), personal resilience is a habit:

> *Whether cultivated through wise mentors, vigorous exercise, access to green space, or a particularly rich relationship with faith, the habits of personal resilience are habits of mind—making them habits we can cultivate and change when armed with the right resources.* (p. 130)

Instinctively, most leaders will say that resilience helps them adopt a positive perspective in the face of adversity. But leadership resilience requires much more than a positive and optimistic disposition. It also requires skills and abilities essential to achieving goals and producing organizational outcomes. Leaders like Amy, as depicted in the leadership resilience scenario above, appear to have a knack for responding to adversity and unexpected change with maturity, equanimity, grace, courage, and pluck. But highly resilient leaders like Amy could not repeatedly face such daunting scenarios and reap the benefits of leadership resilience without experiencing what it feels like to do so. Thankfully, whether or not we become highly resilient leaders, we all possess ordinary resilience, which helps us get our foot in the door. Ordinary resilience helps leaders stay in the game long enough to develop the deeper levels of resilience required by the demands of leadership.

Leadership Resilience: Positively Transformational

Fortified with this foundational understanding that resilience is in fact quite wonderfully ordinary—that most of us are blessed with basic human systems of adaptation that allow us to soldier on in spite of incredible adversity—then what makes leadership resilience different? Why do leaders need to cultivate a type of resilience that is anything more or anything different from ordinary resilience?

The simple answers to these questions are found in the extraordinary demands of leadership within complex, ambiguous, and constantly changing systems. Bottom line: If ordinary resilience is bouncing back and resuming the path one has been on, then leadership resilience is bouncing forward and leading not just oneself, but others, into new and ambiguous realities. Following the famous words of Yogi Berra, who reportedly advised "When you reach a fork in the road, take it," leadership resilience is seen as your ability to make the most of every fork in the road and inspire others to walk with you with confidence.

Faster and Stronger

Given that most people are in fact resilient, it should come as no surprise that most leaders are resilient too. What may be interesting to learn, however, is that some people, including successful leaders, are more resilient than others. In his book *The Resiliency Advantage: Master Change, Thrive Under Pressure, and Bounce Back From Setbacks* (2005), the late Al Siebert compares people who are highly resilient to those who linger or remain in less resilient states, where they feel victimized by the circumstances of life. Siebert writes:

> Highly resilient people are flexible, adapt to new circumstances quickly, and thrive in constant change. Most important, they expect to bounce back and feel confident that they will. They have a knack for creating good luck out of circumstances that many others see as bad luck. (p. 2)

In line with Siebert's observations, my (Elle's) research illuminates similar qualities of highly resilient individuals. Since 2009, I have been looking at data from leaders who complete an inventory that she uses in her leadership consulting practice. The inventory provides a snapshot of an individual's status with regard to certain leadership choices necessary to facilitate sustainable change—perhaps the most challenging demand of leadership. Leadership resilience is one of the choices evaluated in this inventory (the other choices are renewal, resonance, and relationships). You can take the entire online version at www.WisdomOut.com, or you can take the individual assessments provided in this book.

This inventory also asks participants to rate themselves on a scale of 1 to 10 for happiness and meaningful work. It turns out that leaders who rate themselves high on happiness and engagement in meaningful work also score in the "amazingly resilient" category of resilience 70% more often than participants who rate themselves low on happiness and engagement in meaningful work. Effective and happy leaders are so incredibly resilient that they might even appear to others to be immune to the forces of nature. Extraordinarily resilient people do seem to operate with a certain amount of indifference to life's travails (Calhoun & Tedeschi, 2006). These findings, combined with the stories of leadership resilience that I have gathered from my fieldwork, confirm what others are saying about the resilience of successful leaders: They respond faster, stronger, wiser, and with a greater amount of pluck and good cheer than leaders who are not as successful.

The Resilience Inventory

Bearing in mind that resilience can be learned, the following inventory will provide you with a current snapshot of your personal resilience (for a computerized administration of this inventory, go to www.WisdomOut.com). You can take this inventory several times per year—perhaps once every quarter—as a way to focus on different facets of resilience. As an inventory, this tool is not diagnostic nor is it an evaluation or assessment. The inventory is designed to encourage you to engage in personal reflection.

Instructions: Respond to each of the statements in Exercise 1.1 quickly, providing your first impulse as the answer. If you are responding as a team, look at the average response or look at the amount of responses for each number in the range. A response of 10 is the strongest possible agreement, and 1 is the strongest possible disagreement. There are no correct answers. However, the inventory will be most useful to you if you provide the most authentic response, and that is likely to be the first response that comes to mind.

Reflection on Your Score

With a pen or highlighter, flag the sentences below that speak to you for whatever reason. Some sentences may seem right on target. Others might seem off the mark. Don't dismiss the off the mark sentences immediately. Instead, reflect alone or with a trusted person or leadership coach about what they might mean.

Exercise 1.1. Personal Resilience Inventory

Statement	Strongly Disagree								Strongly Agree	
	1	2	3	4	5	6	7	8	9	10
Almost every week, I encounter a situation that is past my breaking point. I don't know if I can bounce back from it.	1	(2)	3	4	5	6	7	8	9	10
When I encounter failure, the causes are almost always factors beyond my control.	1	2	(3)	4	5	6	7	8	9	10
When I suffer professional disappointments, I doubt I can ever make it up to my boss, team, or my organization.	1	(2)	3	4	5	6	7	8	9	10
The last time I suffered a personal loss such as the loss of a friend, partner, or family member, I felt life could never be as good as it once was.	1	2	3	(4)	5	6	7	8	9	10
If I ask for help from colleagues, they will know that I am incapable of doing adequate work on my own.	1	(2)	3	4	5	6	7	8	9	10
When I encounter silence in relationships, it usually means that the other person is disappointed or angry with me.	1	2	3	(4)	5	6	7	8	9	10
When I think of tragic events in the news or in history, most of them were just unavoidable.	1	(2)	3	4	5	6	7	8	9	10
The significant changes that have happened in my life were usually caused by forces outside my control.	1	(2)	3	4	5	6	7	8	9	10
In the past year, I have attempted to make a major personal change, but outside influences prevented me from following through on it.	1	(2)	3	4	5	6	7	8	9	10
In the past year, I have thought about or attempted to make an important professional change, but I could not get the support from organizations and those in charge to make it work.	(1)	2	3	4	5	6	7	8	9	10

Total Score: 24

Interpreting your score

Where do highly resilient leaders tend to score on the Resilience Inventory? Leaders who take the online version of the Resilience Inventory and rate themselves high on happiness and meaningful work score most often in the range of 0–25.

If you scored in the range of 0–25: You are an amazingly resilient person. When you encounter disappointments, you bounce back quickly and you hit the ground running. Likely, you are confident in your ability to learn from experience and feel almost certain that you can influence the results the next time. This doesn't mean you avoid the adversities of life, but you are able to see adversity as an opportunity for growth and change. This strong confidence in your ability and healthy skepticism of the influences of the outside world will generally serve you well. However, others may sometimes see your confidence as indifference to the forces of nature and society. Therefore, you must not forget that others around you may not be as resilient as you are. Find out how you can help to mitigate the impact of adversity for those around you. Ask what they need, and provide resources and emotional support that help others who are less resilient find their way.

If you scored in the range of 26–50: You are a moderately resilient person, fairly confident in your abilities to withstand the slings and arrows of outrageous fortune, or at least of daily life. Your amiability and self-confidence are balanced by a healthy understanding of outside influences on your personal and professional success. In the face of disruption, however, your equanimity is not always balanced with action in response to new realities. Others may interpret this inconsistency as a sign that you do not always see the connection between events and your role in events or in your agency to respond to events. You will benefit from clarifying your analysis of situations and expressing your perceptions to those around you. For example, when you encounter a disappointment, it will be helpful if you articulate clearly where your personal responsibility begins and the impact of outside forces ends, and commit to actions within your circle of influence and control.

If you scored in the range of 51–75: You will benefit from an explicit focus on improving your personal resilience. Your life experiences have influenced your thought patterns in a troubling way, robbing you of confidence in your own abilities to influence your future. This can create a sense of fatalism that becomes a self-fulfilling prophesy. If you think things cannot improve, then they probably will not. If you believe that your influence on events around you is limited, then you will probably be correct. You would benefit from focusing on some very short-term (one- to four-day) objectives in which you can demonstrate your ability to influence your own life and have an impact on events around you. Rather than pursue an overwhelmingly large objective and risk disappointment, consider the pursuit of a series of small victories. The cumulative effect of them might surprise you.

If you scored in the range of 76–100: You have suffered serious personal and professional setbacks, and because you are convinced that these disappointments are beyond your control, you are heading toward a future of despair unless you take serious and immediate corrective action. Your support structures at home and at work may have abandoned you, as your cloud of bleak disappointment tends to scare away those who might try to offer assistance. While you may think that you are simply being open and honest about the way the world is, your views can strike others as bleak and foreboding and therefore even people who care about you do not spend much time around you. That makes for a very lonely and disappointing life, which worsens the cycle of solitude, anger, and cynicism in which you find yourself. Fortunately, there are skills you can develop that will lead to resilience and renewal, but this will require some intense focus and concentration on a daily, or even an hourly, basis. You will need to check your thought patterns for accuracy and engage in resilience exercises that will allow you to demonstrate your impact on your life and on the world around you. You deserve to have a much happier life than you have right now.

More Like Post-traumatic Growth

Resilient leaders also tend to be highly resilient individuals. These individuals sustain an aura of leadership in the face of adversity and they bounce forward quickly; they regain their footing and they hit the ground running. The ability to be highly resilient and bounce forward into new realities makes leadership resilience closer to what we see in the phenomenon known as post-traumatic growth rather than ordinary resilience. Like post-traumatic growth, which involves movement beyond pre-trauma levels of adaptation, leadership resilience has a quality of transformation about it—it is not about staying the same, it is about becoming better as a result of the hardship (Tedeschi & Calhoun, 2004). This is growth that requires a transformed perspective—one that emerges only after assumptions have been challenged, broken down, and revealed. Transformation from adversity is a coveted prize.

Positive Effects of Negative Events

Coined by Tedeschi and Calhoun (1996), the term post-traumatic growth deals with the surprisingly positive effects that come from negative events.

According to Tedeschi and Calhoun, the positive effects resulting from post-traumatic growth show up in five forms:

1. A sense that because of the crisis, new opportunities and possibilities have emerged
2. A greater appreciation for people and warmer relationships with family and friends
3. A greater sense of personal strength, efficacy, and confidence in focusing on goals and accomplishing dreams
4. A greater appreciation for life overall, including a broader philosophy about what matters and a greater sense of fulfillment, meaning, and purpose
5. Deepened spirituality or a significant change in one's belief system

Such is the case of Beth, a charge nurse who got off on the wrong foot with key members of the nursing team she supported, resulting in their request to transfer to other departments. Beth was understandably upset about the situation and recognized the accrued gaffes she made that led to the team's disenchantment with her. Beth says, "Although I can't make the two nurses stay and give me another chance, I can move forward from this point, learn from my mistakes, and be a better leader for the new team coming in." Beth added:

Sure, my confidence was shaken and I was even afraid I might be demoted. But I reached out to the people around me and now I know that the only way to get things accomplished as a leader is through others. The bigger lesson here is that this is exactly what we preach to the staff nurses. It embarrasses me to know that I was not the best role model for working well with others. Thank goodness I have a compassionate manager who wants me to succeed and will coach me through this. She even invited me to come to a panel discussion at a regional conference for novice leaders.

When we analyze Beth's story through the lens of post-traumatic growth, we can see each element at work:

A sense of new possibilities and opportunities. Beth looks forward to being a better leader in her second year. Also, Beth is astonished to find that instead of ostracizing her, her supervisor actually invited her to a conference where she can learn and grow.

Changes in relationships with others. The vulnerability that Beth felt when she found herself facing this leadership challenge caused her to reach out to others. Self-disclosure about the situation and how she feels about it activated a network of people, including her supervisor, who could introduce new and different points of view, which will help her make better future decisions. Beth's willingness to accept help makes her more collaborative, and in Beth's case increases her sensitivity about the importance of relationships overall and especially those with her leadership team.

Perceived change in self with greater efficacy and confidence. Beth expresses feeling more confident and able to act on the lessons she learned. She feels that the way she came through this challenge makes her a better leader. She is more experienced, more self-assured, and feels confident she will face future difficulties with competence, collaboration, and compassion.

Changes in philosophy. Although Beth will not have a second chance with her first leadership team (since two members transferred to different departments), she is deeply appreciative that she has a chance to be a different kind of leader for the new team. When it comes to making leadership decisions now, collaboration with others is at the top of Beth's list.

Deepened spirituality or a significant change in one's belief system. Beth returned to the fundamental values that brought her to the profession of nursing in the first place—her commitment to patients and to doing what is best for them.

Resilient leaders like Beth actually appear to thrive in conditions that bring others down—they become better because of the way they work through each adversity. They value learning in all forms and are especially bolstered by hard-won lessons. These insights do not rest as dormant and interesting pieces of information, they become key tenets for guiding new decisions. Leaders who demonstrate this high level of resilience exemplify the saying "When the going gets tough, the tough get going." This is the sort of leadership resilience that creates opportunity. It is more than steadiness in the face of adversity and stress—it is also the gumption to navigate toward sustaining resources that provide the grit required to actually transform the situation from one of hardship to one of opportunity.

It seems important at this point to emphasize that resilient leaders do not dodge adversity or escape the vagaries of life. Resilient leaders feel pain, become distressed, and some days they go home and cry. But they do exhibit high levels of resilience, and they experience growth from the way they face adversity. They see themselves and others see them as having been made wiser by the challenge and the lessons learned.

The Requirements of Leadership: What Makes Leadership Resilience More Challenging

When it comes to resilience, leaders bear a great responsibility. In the face of adversity, leaders must exhibit high levels of resilience to segue the resulting momentum into growth and change, not just for themselves, but for the entire organization. Management expert Tom Peters even links behaviors that are decidedly resilient to the development of trust: "[a]s a subordinate, I trust a leader who shows up, makes the tough calls, takes the heat, sleeps well amidst the furor, and then aggressively chomps into the next task in the morning with visible vitality" (2001). As we saw through Amy's leadership resilience story at the start of this chapter, the resilience of the leader influences the resilience of the people they lead. Like Amy, leaders must regain their leadership footing quickly, while simultaneously leading forward into emerging and ambiguous realities.

The requirements of leadership resilience are great, but ultimately, leadership resilience produces outcomes and benefits that make the challenge worthwhile. Before reading the list of benefits in the box below, take a minute to jot down your own list. What do you believe are the benefits of leadership resilience, both to you and to your organization? How do your ideas compare with the list provided in the box "What Leadership Resilience Produces."

The Vicissitudes of Complex Organizations

During times of adversity and change, leaders face strong organizational forces that create drag and make resilience development a priority. Resistance to these antagonistic forces is futile and even counterproductive. They are inherent to complex organizations and may even serve to create a level of suffering necessary to transformational change and post-traumatic growth. The best a leader can do is expect them, embrace them, and understand them. Consider this list of organizational forces that make resilience a leadership priority:

1. You usually have little transition time between the challenging event and your next move—even when your next move is to mindfully take a step back and gather additional information.

2. Progress must continue. You are expected to manage goals upward to achieve new levels of performance. This is true even when the resources you've depended on change, or are reduced or eliminated.

3. You must lead others, many of whom are resistant to change, not through control and coercion, but through influence.

4. The shared purpose and vision of the organization is yoked to your resilience—a reality that requires you to develop deep understanding about what it takes to promote organizational learning and growth.

5. People expect more from leaders. Leaders must adhere to higher standards and expectations. Maladaptive responses during times of adversity open you to criticism and diminish your reputation.

6. Your own sense of loss and disillusionment may be very great indeed. Even so, you must manage your own emotions and help the people around you manage theirs.

7. The previous reality no longer exists or has been significantly altered. Therefore, to force a return to a previous existence is unhelpful and lacks courage. It is illusionary—not visionary.

8. More often than not, you must step into new or emerging realities, and must therefore leverage resources for contexts that are still undefined, unstable, and ambiguous.

9. In order to take advantage of the opportunities that emerge with change, you need to be more open to learning and be more open to having your assumptions and schemas changed.

What Leadership Resilience Produces

1. A proactive way to respond to disruptive change, challenges, and adversity.

2. Perspectives that help leaders manage the stress that naturally occurs around change initiatives.

3. A culture of achievement with sustained focus on patient well-being and organizational outcomes.

4. Leaders who accomplish tasks and are seen as trustworthy. When resilience leaders say they are going to do something, they stick with it and they follow through on nitty-gritty details, building their reputations as trustworthy leaders.

5. A cultural example for the next generation of leaders. Leadership resilience creates a template for how the organization and community responds to adversity.

6. Persistence in problem solving that often leads to breakthrough thinking, creativity, ingenuity, and innovation.

7. Visible leadership. Controversies and challenges are defining moments for leaders. People watch how leaders respond during times of adversity and form enduring impressions that will define the leaders from that point forward.

The Stresses of Nurse Leadership: Neither Rare Nor Unusual

Adversity is neither rare nor unusual. When Robert, a nurse manager of the emergency department in a large northeastern hospital thinks back to his first year and a half as a novice nurse manager, he has to agree. Here are just a few of the disruptive challenges that in many ways were the crucibles of Robert's first management experience:

- Two nurses who reported to Robert were accused of stealing controlled medications.
- Robert became impatient with a new nurse and reprimanded her in front of a patient. The nurse filed a complaint against him.
- A special needs patient fell in the bathroom and although not seriously hurt, was quite terrified and was inconsolable.
- One of the best nurses on the team was diagnosed with cancer. While she was undergoing chemotherapy and focused on her recovery, her colleagues missed her and felt great concern for her health.
- Long waits in the emergency room led to low patient satisfaction scores and a higher than normal percentage of patients leaving before being seen by a healthcare provider.
- Robert observed that certain physicians ordered tests unlikely to change the outcome for the patient. Unfortunately, this practice contributed to lags in patient disposition.

To be sure, joy characterized Robert's first year as nurse manager much more than hardship ever could, but these examples emphasize the truth in the statement that disruptive change is neither unusual nor rare. As Minnesota nurse leader Megan Damon says, the challenges nurse leaders face *is* the work of nurse leadership.

Given the subjectivity of the causes of leadership distress—what one leader finds traumatic, another might view as part and parcel to the job—not to mention the fast pace of change, it is impossible to fully enumerate and describe every adversity facing nurse leaders now or in the future. We can, however, identify the broad categories of such adversities and provide examples. Table 1.1 shows types and examples of adversities faced by nurse leaders. Some adversities are seismic to nurse leaders as human beings and within their leadership role. Other adversities are inherent to the work, yet still could be perceived by individuals as either traumatic or passé, depending on the leader's capacity for resilience.

TABLE 1.1. **Potential Adversities Facing Nurse Leaders**

Chronic Stress Stemming From the Daily Churn of Leadership
• Minimal time to make decisions
• Overload of tasks
• Technology and equipment failures
• Interruptions and urgent requests
• Miscommunications and misunderstandings
• Not knowing how to manage requests
• Feeling overwhelmed, overloaded, and unproductively busy
• Lacking a skill or a key piece of information
• Misreading a situation and needing to backpedal
Chronic Personal Stress
• Lack of sleep, exhaustion
• Poor nutrition or lack of time to eat and replenish fluids
• Muscle strains and physical pain
Personal and Interpersonal Leadership Gauntlets
• People not working well together. Difficult interpersonal relationships
• Patient and/or family concerns about peers, colleagues, and the people you supervise
• Receiving unexpected, negative feedback
• Not knowing how to provide constructive feedback to others
• Being unprepared for a meeting, conversation, or presentation
• Learning that you acted on incorrect or incomplete information
• Showing poor judgment or making decisions that had unintended and negative impacts
• Being dressed down publicly
• Collegial isolation
• Being the target of a bully, backstabber, liar, gossiper, or someone who takes credit for your work
• Helping people balance authority/responsibility discrepancies
• Increased patient acuity
Chronic Organizational Stress
• Staffing shortages
• Lack of clarity in directions and expectations
• Changes in technology
• Changes in policies and procedures
• Procedures and processes that create hoops to jump through and delay progress
• Timeline breeches
• Responding to pay for performance measures

- Data showing inconsistent patient outcomes
- Breaches of safety, protocol, and norms
- Unproductive meetings
- Resistance to implementing the strategies of the organization
- Stakeholder resistance to change
- Anxiety in the face of implementation dips
- Persistent low scores in patient/family/community/employee satisfaction
- Budget cuts
- Introduction of new laws, rules, and regulations
- Having to let go or pink slip peers, colleagues, and staff
- Having to reduce resources to programs and people
- Being the bearer of information that people find upsetting
- Being placed on an improvement list by an external standard board
- Loss of resources and support for programs
- Being reassigned
- Losing a team member to reassignment
- Miscommunications and misunderstandings between key people and groups
- Labor grievances
- Loss of support from key stakeholders
- Unpleasant physical workplace environments

Acute Organizational Shocks

- Acts of violence in the workplace
- The unexpected and sudden death of a patient
- Becoming aware of illegal or unethical behavior of a colleague
- Hurricanes, tornadoes, and other natural disasters
- Terrorism
- Intruder violence
- The sudden and unexpected death of a colleague
- Bullying
- Discrimination
- Criminal charges against colleagues

Moral Distress

- Balancing the values of team members with the needs of the organization
- Facing organizational practices that do not support personal values regarding patient care, families, employees, communities
- Feeling regret due to choosing not to act in accordance with personal values
- Feeling and believing that you lack moral strength as a person or as a leader
- Personal indiscretions that come to light

(CONTINUED)

TABLE 1.1. **Potential Adversities Facing Nurse Leaders (continued)**

Potentially Shattering Personal/Professional Gauntlets
• Being in an abusive relationship
• You or a family member becomes seriously ill
• Divorce or death of a family member
• Being fired for cause
• Having your contract non-renewed
• Facing a personal or work-related lawsuit
• Alcohol or other addictions that come to light on the job or in the community
• Being arrested or receiving a DUI
• Being accused or found guilty of a crime
• Being accused or found guilty of violating harassment laws

Nurse leaders are no different from the general population, and their resilience has much to do with how they perceive and choose to frame the adversities they face. For any one of the educational leadership adversities presented in Table 1.1, leaders can choose to respond with resilience.

Clearly, not all of the challenges that hit nursing leaders need to have a seismic emotional impact. Many would still agree that a leader's perception and response to stress, loss, crisis, and challenge is personal and highly subjective. What acts as a devastating blow to one nurse leader may be perceived by another as an expected or even interesting development. The fact still remains that highly resilient leaders tend to credit the most difficult circumstances and phases in their lives with giving them the skills and experience they need to handle the demands of the future.

Moving on to Chapter 2: A Model of Leadership Resilience

What we've established in this first chapter is that when it comes to leadership during times of adversity and unexpected change, bouncing back is not an option. Leaders must bounce forward. They must regain their footing quickly and simultaneously inspire action within new realities. Moreover, leaders must transform the hardships they face into growth and change for themselves and for the organization. Drawing on ideas from leadership, resilience, and post-traumatic growth, in the next chapter we'll explore a model that describes a way to do this.

2

A Model for
Resilient Leadership

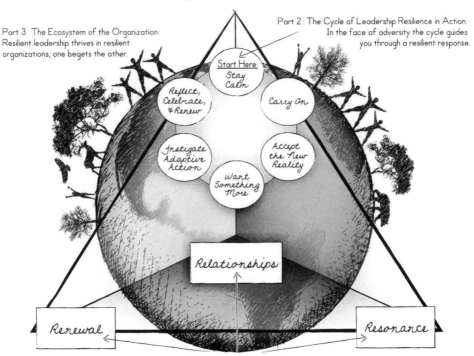

Leadership Resilience Model

Part 3: The Ecosystem of the Organization: Resilient leadership thrives in resilient organizations; one begets the other.

Part 2: The Cycle of Leadership Resilience in Action: In the face of adversity the cycle guides you through a resilient response.

Start Here: Stay Calm

Reflect, Celebrate, & Renew

Carry On

Instigate Adaptive Action

Accept the New Reality

Want Something More

Relationships

Renewal

Resonance

Part 1: The Three Leadership Resilience Enabling Capacities: Your ability to take resilient action depends on the enabling capacities. Care for them well!

FIGURE 2.1 **The Wisdom Out Leadership Resilience Model and its Three Parts**

If ordinary resilience is the ability to bounce back to previous levels of functioning with little emotional, physical, and psychological fallout, then leadership resilience is the ability to bounce forward into change. The good news is that bouncing forward does not just create benefits in your leadership work. The very traits that make you a resilient leader will also enrich your life.

The Leadership Resilience Model

Theoretical models make visible our tacit assumptions and beliefs about how the world works. However, as we change and as the world around us changes, our assumptions and beliefs should also evolve. Thus, over time, theoretical models become outmoded and need revision; as George Box famously said, "All models are wrong but some are useful" (Box & Draper, 1987, p. 424). To the extent that they are relevant and useful, theoretical models give us a way to understand universal human experiences. In the spirit of accepting both the limitations and the opportunities of theoretical models, the Wisdom Out Leadership Resilience Model presented in this chapter draws out the salient features of leadership resilience and is derived from research data gathered from nurses in practice over the past 12 years.

The Model, depicted in Figure 2.1, has three parts:

- **Part 1**. A tetrahedron anchored on the three corners by the enabling capacities of leadership resilience: Relationships, Resonance, and Renewal.
- **Part 2**. A non-directional cycle inside the tetrahedron showing the six Leadership Resilience Actions: Stay Calm, Carry On, Accept the New Reality, Want Something More, Instigate Adaptive Action, and Reflect, Celebrate, and Renew.
- **Part 3**. An outer circle that represents the larger ecosystem of the organization the leader works within, such as teams different levels in an organization or the nursing profession as a whole.

Taken together, the three parts of the Wisdom Out Leadership Resilience Model describe a practice of leadership resilience. A brief explanation of each part of the model will aid you as you reflect on Figure 2.1.

Model Part 1—The Leadership Resilience-Enabling Capacities: Renewal, Relationships, and Resonance

The tetrahedron at the center of the model is anchored on each corner by three leadership resilience-enabling capacities: Relationships, Resonance, and Renewal. The three leadership resilience-enabling capacities fuel resilient actions in leaders when they find themselves in the midst of disruptive change. Think of the enabling capacities as personal, sustainable, and long-term resources that empower leaders to quickly ramp up and respond with leadership resilience when it is needed. Chapters 3 through 5 explore the three enabling capacities of the model in more detail. Detailed below is a brief description and discussion of the major foundational concepts of the model:

> **Renewal.** Resilient nurse leaders purposefully feed their personal, social, and professional beings. They have identified what creates energy for them so they can show up for their lives and for the important work they do. Resilient leaders tend to gain energy from doing meaningful work and so they mindfully balance life and work so they can do the work they love, for as long as they wish.
>
> **Relationships.** In the context of leadership resilience, relationships refer to the connected social networks of people and organizations that support leaders and the work of leaders. These networks and connections mobilize resources and support to leaders at times of adversity. Leaders with strong and diverse networks find support when they need it the most.
>
> **Resonance.** Leaders with high levels of resonance have the ability to move people to action. Resonant leaders have mastered the skills of emotional intelligence. They regulate their emotions well, which in turn helps others do the same. In the aftermath of adversity, the effect of leadership resonance creates an environment where insightful action is possible.

Antifragility and the Leadership Resilience Model

Leaders who intentionally and mindfully develop and cultivate the three leadership resilience-enabling capacities increase their "antifragility"—a term coined by Nicholas Taleb from the New York Polytechnic Institute in Brooklyn. Taleb strongly contrasts antifragility with resilience: "Antifragility is beyond resilience or robustness. The resilient resists shock and stays the same; the antifragile gets better" (2012, p. 3). Taleb says that fragility and antifragility are degrees on a spectrum and both can be detected "using a simple test of asymmetry: anything that has more upside than downside from random events (or certain shocks) is antifragile; the reverse is fragile" (p. 5). The transformational nature of leadership resilience has much in common with Taleb's premise. The enabling capacities of renewal, relationships, and resonance increase a leader's ability to be wiser, stronger, and more relevant in the aftermath of disruptive change. The enabling capacities cultivated by resilient leaders create upsides to adverse events.

Model Part 2—Leadership Resilience in Action

Consider the second part of the Wisdom Out Leadership Resilience Model. At the center of the tetrahedron is the six-step cycle of Leadership Resilience in Action. Based on research over time, resilient leaders consistently activated these six strategies in response to the adversities that befall them and the systems they lead. The steps and strategies are: Stay Calm, Carry On, Accept the New Reality, Want Something More, Instigate Adaptive Action, and Reflect, Celebrate, and Renew. Chapters 7 through 12 will describe and discuss each of these steps and strategies in more detail and provide examples of how resilient leaders behave, activate, and model the strategies in difficult and challenging situations. The non-directional continuous cycle implies that a leader's resilient response to adversity requires execution of the six actions most often in the order presented, with the option of returning to a previous action as needed.

Understandably, some might perceive a cycle as rigid and overly constraining. At the same time, most agree that the actions presented in the cycle cumulatively initiate and complete a resilient response—one that is visible to anyone watching the leader as he or she faces adversity. Thus, the presentation of a simple cycle of action isolates important aspects of what in reality is a complex and intuitive response, and allows us to study them.

The leadership resilience actions offer a helpful framework for how to respond to challenges and adversities as a leader. The actions also describe how a leader becomes more resilient—for growth does not occur as a direct result of challenges, but in the struggle with the new reality in the aftermath of the challenge (Tedeschi & Calhoun, 2004).

The events that trigger the Leadership Resilience in Action cycle usually are not the single, small annoyances that populate most days. Instead, they are events that test your assumptive world (Tedeschi & Calhoun, 2004). Events that trigger resilience are the disruptive changes or disorienting dilemmas that cause you to rethink ideas and return to the drawing board. Difficult as they are, these events also hold the most promise for transformational change (Mezirow, 2000).

When adversity strikes, Leadership Resilience in Action (Part 2 of the model) draws on the three enabling capacities of relationships, resonance, and renewal (Part 1 of the model). When the enabling capacities are robust, leaders are more able to respond to adversity with agility and grace. As an additional benefit, leaders who activate the resilience actions become engaged in active problem solving, which is a strategy for coping with adversity and is related to positive long-term outcomes (Butler et al., 2005). As one nurse from a hospital in Oregon says,

People will imply or outright tell you that something cannot be done. Knowing that there is a cycle of resilience in action gives me a strategy for problem solving—especially when people tell you that something cannot be done. When I think about my personal resilience in action, I feel I have a way to look at what is standing in our way, with the idea that maybe this is something that in fact can be done.

Model Part 3—The Ecosystem of the Organization and the Profession of Nursing

The third part of the Wisdom Out Leadership Resilience Model is the outer circle represented by the image of the earth, which symbolizes the organization: the ecosystem and contexts in which the leader exerts influence and participates in the greater communities in which they work and the profession of nursing. The relationship between resilient leadership and resilient organizations is highly reciprocal. Resilient leaders create resilient organizations, and in turn, resilient organizations cultivate, nurture, and sustain resilient leaders. It is here, against the scrim of complex healthcare organizations and cultures, that leaders have the opportunity to grow in resilience.

In its broadest terms, the organization and its prevailing culture are also the source of the very same challenges that make resilience so necessary to nurse leadership. Resilient organizations do not escape adversity and disruptive change, but the more resilient the organization, the more challenges look like opportunities. As you will learn in Part IV, resilient leaders do not shy away from creating necessary disruption. They get out in front of adversity by engaging the system in challenging conversations that question assumptions and invite disorder.

Key Assumptions of the Leadership Resilience Model

Drawing on research from the fields of leadership, change theory, organizational learning, emotional intelligence, resilience, and post-traumatic growth, the Wisdom Out Leadership Resilience Model is founded on several key assumptions:

1. Relationships, resonance, and renewal shore up and enable leadership resilience.
   a. Leaders can't go it alone. Other people are important to their success
   b. Optimism, vision, and compassion for oneself and others create a powerful emotional force field that infuses hope, possibility, and a can-do perspective during times of disruptive change.

    c. Leaders need personal energy to sustain their focus and ability to bounce forward. They need to find what renews them, and they need to engage in those activities.

2. Leaders who continually nurture relationships, resonance, and renewal more easily activate and draw down stores of resilience when in the throes of disruptive change.

3. Leadership resilience is an inside-out job. Resilient leaders create resilient organizations.

4. It helps us to look at the development of leadership resilience and what resilient leaders do. We can become more resilient ourselves through learning from those who have been resilient.

5. Resilience builds more resilience, out of which comes insight and wisdom to apply to future adversities.6. Resilience is a discipline that must be practiced. Every moment offers a new chance to practice the actions of resilience.

Benefits of The Leadership Resilience Model

The Wisdom Out Leadership Resilience Model described in this book offers nurses several benefits that make them more effective, balanced, and joyful leaders:

- It provides a way for you to act with leadership resilience—to bounce forward, not just simply return to a previous level of functioning while you simultaneously create resilient organizations that breed leadership resilience in others.

- It is aspirational and inspirational. It strives to convey ideal states of functioning and multiple pathways toward leadership resilience.

- It helps you assess your strengths and weaknesses in leadership resilience. It presents a desirable vision that you can compare yourself to and work toward.

- It asserts that you can become more resilient; therefore, it poses both a challenge and a quest. Will you make up your mind to grow in resilience? Will you commit to a lifelong practice of leadership resilience?

- It will challenge other paradigms you might hold that are less helpful because they reinforce the idea that resilience is difficult and unattainable or that it is not something an individual can learn.

- It allows you to explore and talk about leadership resilience with interest, curiosity, and minimal defensiveness. You can look honestly at the concept of leadership resilience while reflecting on your own leadership resilience.

- It challenges you to overcome the limitations that constrain your leadership resilience and it offers a blueprint for growth.

A Brief Word About Crisis Response

To be clear, the leadership resilience actions found at the center of the model are not the same thing as a crisis response plan. A crisis response plan describes and details macro procedures and decision points in response to a crisis such as severe weather, intruders, and other emergencies. In the aftermath of any one of these events, however, the Leadership Resilience Model and the ideas in this book become useful tools for you to employ.

Using the Model: A Disciplined Practice

With the hope that you gain all the benefits it offers both personally and professionally, we invite you to think of leadership resilience as a disciplined practice and not as a goal you need to achieve. As a practice, leadership resilience clearly is not a prepackaged single technique, magic bullet, or specific formula. It is unlikely that such a single solution exists! In the long run, however, treating leadership resilience as a practice is far more powerful and sustainable than any one technique could ever be. As a practice, you realize you have a lifetime to become more resilient. If you mess it up one day, you have the next day—really, the next minute—to get back into the practice.

Over time, leaders who practice resilience gain a resilient presence; they believe they are resilient, and others see them as resilient. With use, the behaviors of leadership resilience will strengthen and become integrated into your leadership skill set and will manifest as a part of who you are and how you act given the contexts of your leadership challenges.

II

The Three Leadership Resilience-Enabling Capacities

Chapter 3. Renewal: Energy for Meaningful Work

Chapter 4. Resonance: Great Leaders Move Us

Chapter 5. Relationships: Surround Yourself with Good Souls

3

Renewal
Energy for Meaningful Work

This is your world. Shape it, or someone else will.

—Gary Lew

Helen is a nurse supervisor who, in addition to her leadership responsibilities, cares for a reduced number of patients in a large urban hospital serving a primarily low-income community, with a high incidence of heart disease and diabetes. She often works twelve-hour shifts and always goes the extra mile to fill in when other nurses need a hand. Helen has worked hard to establish rapport with the nurses she supervises, some of whom were not exactly friendly to her when she first accepted her position, replacing a veteran nurse who had been their peer for two decades. She learned early on that many of the nurses in her unit were particularly sensitive about being asked to do work they felt was outside of their realm of responsibility. Many of them seemed to have lost their zeal for nursing as a profession, and certainly, as demonstrated by their lack of involvement in new initiatives and committees, were disengaged from the mission of the hospital. For these nurses, dealing with the patients assigned to them was their job and they resented anything that interfered with completing their tasks as efficiently as possible.

Helen responded to what she called their "grumpiness" by avoiding asking her nurses to do anything above and beyond. She had become fearful about delegating, identifying strengths in others, and involving them in new challenges that would help them grow. As a result, not only was her unit lacking in innovation and leadership, but Helen herself was rapidly feeling the effects of burnout. The responsibility Helen felt to her community and to the hospital to improve healthcare quality while reducing healthcare costs was great. She knew that accomplishing these goals would require the ingenuity and energy achieved only through collaboration. Yet she had never felt more alone.

On the home front, Helen, a single parent of two middle-school-aged kids, was facing another challenge. Her son was becoming increasingly withdrawn from school and family. His long spells of isolation up in his room playing video games were interrupted only by minimal grunts at meal times and frequent eruptions of anger directed at Helen and at his younger sister. Almost every day while at work, Helen's daughter calls her in tears, begging her to come home.

Lately, Helen has bouts of heartburn that no longer respond to the antacid tablets she regularly pops into her mouth. And although she is exhausted, sleep eludes her. She climbs into bed at night but then lies awake ruminating unproductively over the events of the day. Her sister has noticed Helen's weight gain; at least twenty pounds over the last year. When her sister encouraged her to join the gym and to go on a healthy diet, Helen snapped back, "I'm a nurse, so obviously I don't need you to tell me about healthy living!"

The Need for Renewal

Helen's predicament is unfortunately all too familiar to nurse leaders everywhere. Ironically, although nurses are the most influential when it comes to patient satisfaction and are valued as the most trustworthy of all healthcare professionals, a 2013 Gallup poll shows that compared to physicians, nurses exercise less, smoke more, and have a higher incidence of diabetes, depression, and high blood pressure. Simultaneously, many work environments for nurses are, in fact, stress generators—lacking in opportunities for collaboration, shared decision-making, meaningful relationships, recognition, and influencing decisions.

Couple these personal and organizational factors with the important requirements of initiatives such as the Triple Aim, which calls for improved healthcare outcomes, better health for specific populations, and decreased healthcare spending (Berwick, Nolan, & Whittington, 2008), the demands on nurse leaders have never been higher. In order to meet these demands, personal and professional renewal must receive equal prioritization.

Without renewal, nurse leaders forfeit the "good life," what career coaches Richard Leider and David Shapiro (2002) describe as "living in the place you belong, with the people you love, doing the right work, on purpose" (p. 29). Failure to attend to these aspects of the good life often results in wrestling with what Leider and Shapiro call the four deadly fears:

1. Fear of having lived a meaningless life
2. Fear of being alone
3. Fear of being lost
4. Fear of dying

Leadership requires mastery of one's self, mastery of communication, mastery of relationships, and mastery of multiple ways of being, thinking, feeling, doing, and influencing in order to transform problems into desired outcomes. Nurses certainly need to develop skill sets related to influence and leading (Sullivan, 2013, Pesut, 2001; 2007; 2008), and these skills must also include mastering the art of personal and professional renewal. As nurse leader Cathy Coleman from the University of San Francisco says. "If you want to inspire trust, you have to be able to chomp into the work of the day. To do this, you need to create a good balance between work and life."

As past president of the Honor Society of Nursing, Sigma Theta Tau International, Dan underscored the importance of renewal through his presidential call to action: Create the future through renewal. He summarized his thoughts about the value and importance of renewal with the following logic:

> As self is renewed, commitments to service come forward more easily. Renewed commitments to service require attention to mindfulness and reflective practice. Mindful reflective practice begets questions that support inquiry. Inquiry guides knowledge work and evidence-based care giving. Care giving supports society as knowledge, values, and service intersect. Knowledgeable people and especially knowledgeable nurses provide care that society needs. Creating a caring society is the spirit work of nursing. Creating a caring society starts with nurses caring for themselves and becoming more conscious and intentional in their being, thinking, feeling, doing, and acting. Reflection is a form of "inner work" that results in the energy for engaging in "outer service." Reflection in-and-on action supports meaning-making and purpose management in one's professional life. (Honor Society of Nursing, Sigma Theta Tau International Scholarship of Reflective Practice Resource Paper, 2005)

There is wisdom in renewal (Pesut, 2008) that requires personal reflection and working through personal issues (Pesut, 2001) as well as the challenges of interdisciplinary healthcare teamwork (Pesut, 2012).

Fundamentally, personal, professional, and social renewal is an inside-out job that begins with awareness. The following inventory gives the reader an opportunity to reflect renewal. As with all inventories in this book, it offers a tool for self-reflection.

The Renewal Inventory

Before reading on, take a few moments to respond to the Renewal Inventory (to take the online version, visit www.WisdomOut.com) depicted in Exercise 3.1, which will provide you with objective feedback about your current state of renewal.

Instructions: Respond to each of the following statements in Exercise 3.1 quickly, providing your first impulse as the answer. If you are responding as a team, look at the average response or look at the amount of responses for each number in the range. A response of 10 is the strongest possible agreement, and 1 is the strongest possible disagreement. There are no correct answers.

Exercise 3.1. Renewal Inventory

Statement	Strongly Disagree								Strongly Agree	
1. Even if I'm meeting my usual goals and being very efficient on my job, I'm not completely fulfilled unless I am achieving a higher purpose serving the greater good.	1	2	3	4	5	6	7	8	9	(10)
2. I can think of several times when, after undergoing adversity, I'm actually better off after the adversity than I was before it.	1	2	3	4	5	6	7	8	9	(10)
3. I can identify very specifically the source of my greatest inspiration.	1	2	3	4	5	6	7	8	9	(10)
4. When I need physical renewal, I know of specific and consistent activities and routines that will be helpful for me.	1	2	3	4	5	6	7	8	(9)	(10)
5. I am very aware of when I need renewal and I know the warning signs that suggest to me that I need support and renewal.	1	2	3	4	(5)	6	7	8	9	10
6. I am able to reflect on my past and think about mistakes I have made without being obsessed and overwhelmed by them. I know my lessons learned and can apply them to my daily life.	1	2	3	4	5	6	7	8	9	(10)
7. I have forgiven myself for my past mistakes.	1	2	3	4	5	6	7	(8)	9	10
8. When I need emotional renewal, I know of people and practices that help me gain renewal.	1	2	3	4	(5)	6	7	8	9	10
9. I have forgiven others, even those who have hurt me very deeply.	1	2	3	4	5	6	7	8	(9)	10
10. I can think of a specific example when I have helped to provide renewal to a colleague or a loved one within the past week	1	2	3	4	(5)	6	7	8	9	10

Total Score: ___80___

Interpreting Your Score

Where do highly resilient leaders tend to score on the Renewal Inventory? Leaders who take the online version of the Renewal Inventory, and who also rate themselves high on happiness and meaningful work, score most often in the range of 71–100.

If You Score in the Range of 10–40: You are so emotionally and physically exhausted it's amazing that you have the energy to read this book. The physical, emotional, and mental challenges you face all run together, and the effects may be showing up in your sleep and eating habits. Even a walk around the block can feel like an insurmountable challenge to you. Most of all, you are very alone. You can be in a crowd in Times Square, among family and friends who care about you, or lying on your couch into the 10th hour of a television and ice cream marathon—it doesn't matter. It's all the same feeling of isolation and despair. You need a break—in every sense of the word—and the sooner you make the break from this landscape of disease, the sooner you will begin the road to renewal.

If You Score in the Range of 41–70: In a nutshell, although you may know how to renew, you may have difficulty taking action. Although you occasionally find new energy, it sometimes feels as if you are treading water in the middle of a vast ocean and there isn't much for you to hang on to when the waves crash around you. Perhaps the most disconcerting statement that others make when they refer to your successes at work or your apparently happy personal life is that you've "got it all." But there are days when the successes on which other people focus offer little or no fulfillment to you. Promotions and raises come and go, and you accept congratulations with little real enthusiasm. When your friends and colleagues express envy of you, you are thinking, "If you only knew how little this means to me." There are exceptions, of course, as you consider moments of physical, emotional, and mental renewal in the past. You sometimes think about re-creating those moments, but transforming thought into action is inconsistent and distant.

If You Score in the Range of 71–100: You have found the sources of renewal in your life and you regularly use them, and this gives you the energy you need to show up for your life. Although you can certainly be effective in your professional life and you are capable of maintaining and sustaining meaningful personal relationships, you find true meaning in service and a contribution to the greater good. You are not superhuman, but you seem to have a level of calm and equanimity that allows you to keep your cool when other people around you panic. You have faced disappointment and loss, and you endure not through blind stoicism but through renewal. When your body and spirit are down, you show the wisdom to stop, rest, and restore yourself, meeting your mental, physical, and spiritual needs. As successful as you are, you are the first to acknowledge that you have not achieved this success alone. You are regularly aware of the role that other people—today and in history—have played in your success. Although you rarely claim credit for it, your personal example serves as sources of renewal for other people.

Reflection on Your Score
Take a moment to reflect on the results of your Renewal Inventory.

My Renewal Inventory Score is: _____

Highlight key insights from the score interpretation you received. What sounds right to you? What seems off? What goals do you want to set for yourself or for your team?

How Renewal Enables Leadership
If you were to read this paragraph while holding your breath, in a matter of seconds you would be acutely aware of the urge to breathe. The uncomfortable sensation you will feel, known as air hunger, is triggered not as you might expect by a lack of oxygen, but by high levels of carbon dioxide accumulating in your blood. Ordinarily you do not need to think about breathing. Unsolicited by your conscious mind, the respiratory control center located in your brain stem monitors your carbon dioxide levels, and when they are out of whack, orders your breathing muscles to take in air. Luckily, normal breathing is an automated function of the human body.

Though more subtle (and therefore, significantly more dangerous), the absence of renewal in leadership also creates a sensation of need, experienced as vague feelings of edginess, restlessness, and the sense that life just is not all that it could be. Unfortunately, many leaders ignore these negative sensations, and because it can take years before their accumulated effects take a toll (often dramatically in the form of heart disease, car accidents, addictions, depression, or divorce), they do not take steps to build in a regular practice of renewal. Some leaders even go so far as to expect to suffer from the demands of leadership. They believe that giving up exercise, play, sleep, relaxation, and family is fair collateral for doing the work they have chosen to do. Leaders who buy into this narrative fail to see the connection between renewal and the ability to lead with stamina, creativity, and joy—qualities that signal resilience. Yet, as we saw in the opening story about Helen, nurses who clearly know what to do to live well often fail to apply what they know in their own lives.

In his book *Predictably Irrational: The Hidden Forces That Shape Our Destiny* (2010), behavioral economist Dan Ariely writes about the research of Ralph Keeney, including the alarming information that premature deaths of people aged 15–64 have increased from 5% in 1900 to 55% in 2000—mostly due to poor personal choices such as overeating, smoking, unsafe sex, sedentary lifestyle, and driving without a seatbelt. Ariely adds the estimation that "about half of us will make a lifestyle decision that will lead us to an early grave" (p. 166).

A persistent lack of renewal does more than diminish your health and lifespan. In organizations, a lack of renewal puts people on a path toward burnout, which, according to the 2007–2008 Towers Perrin survey of nearly 90,000 employees worldwide, is the leading cause of employee disengagement—a condition that most certainly undermines leadership resilience (Perrin, 2008). Employee engagement is seen in individuals that are psychologically invested in contributing to the mission and goals of their organizations. Unfortunately, worldwide and across industries, a 2012 Gallup poll (Crabtree, 2013) shows only 13% of employees are engaged in their jobs. Astonishingly, 63% of individuals are not engaged and 24% are actively disengaged. These burned out, unengaged, and actively disengaged individuals can stall or prevent resilient leaderships and organizations.

Feel Better, Think Better

Personal renewal is important for your health and well-being—it allows you to show up for your life, and it gives you energy to do meaningful work. But doing things that make you feel good and give you energy can also make you think better. Renewal provides you with the interludes you need to solve complex problems with creativity.

For example, Lisa McDonald, an orthopedic surgical nurse in New York state, who is also a runner and triathlete, says, "When I'm stressed and I go for a run, I figure things out." Running is especially helpful for Lisa when she is trying to figure out how to persuasively present new ideas to her teammates. She says:

> When I've been told no about something I think is a good idea, I realize that even though I see the need clearly, I need to do a better job of multiplying the number of people who see what I see. I go for a run and I figure out how to bring the idea back again in a different way.

Interludes of Renewal

If your natural tendency is to adopt a workaholic approach to life, not only are you jeopardizing your health, but you might actually be preventing the breakthrough thinking you desire and need. Consider that a 2009 study from the Center for Creative Leadership finds that many high-flying founders and executives also engage in regular physical exercise. For these leaders, taking time off to hit the gym contributed to their success. Other leaders gain the same kind of energy from cooking, gardening, seeing all of the Sundance Film Festival films, rescuing greyhound dogs, or dressing up as Brad Majors, the hero from *The Rocky Horror Picture Show* and attending weekly midnight screenings.

Dr. Fredrick Hudson's 1999 research on the topic of renewal reveals self-renewing adults are value driven, connected to the world around them, relish solitude and quiet, pace themselves and enjoy contact with nature, are creative and playful, adapt to change, learn from down times, focus on the future and never stop learning. Children seem to instinctively know that interludes of renewal make you think better. At The Tinkering School in California, for example, kids gather for two weeks at a time to invent. They are given access to raw supplies and tools, and work with a team to invent something mechanical. In a 2009 TED Talk, Gever Tulley, camp founder and director, said he notices that the kids do something rather amazing when they run into a quandary with their inventions: they get down on their bellies and they decorate them. Tulley said, "It is here, in these interludes, that the kids have the breakthrough thoughts. The interludes provide periods of time for conceptual incubation."

Leaders in fields other than nursing also offer insight about how to create interludes of renewal for themselves. For former school superintendent Carmella Franco, renewal comes in quiet contemplation at the end of the day, often in the garden or walking alone. Franco says:

> When I feel the heavy thoughts of the day come down on me, I simply make up my mind not to ruminate on the negative. Instead I move on to more solution-oriented thoughts. I jot a few words down and leave them out where I can see them. Then, as I garden or walk or just sit quietly and relax, the answer comes to me.

When the best answer comes to Franco it often feels like a eureka moment. She says, "When the answer comes and it feels right, I know it holds the insight I need.

No matter what personal renewal you decide to take part in, the most important thing is that you use the resulting energy to show up for your life and take advantage of all of the opportunities and challenges that life brings. The trick is to have the discipline to leave the task at hand when your mind is stuck, and engage in interludes of renewal.

Inspired Thought

Steven Johnson, author of the book *Where Good Ideas Come From: The Natural History of Innovation* (2010), tells the story of Stephane Tarnier, an obstetrician living in Paris in the late 1870s. One day, Dr. Tarnier took a day off from work to go to the zoo. Lingering at an exhibit of newly hatched chicks, tumbling about inside a heated box, Dr. Tarnier suddenly saw how the same concept could also work for human newborns. In no time at all, the good doctor hired the zoo poultry raiser to build a similar device for the hospital. Once installed and in use, Dr. Tarnier went on to conduct crucial research to prove that the incubator could save the lives of ailing and premature infants. Thank goodness Dr. Tarnier took a day off to go to the zoo!

The stories of Dr. Tarnier and other leaders provide evidence that renewal does more than create energy to get through the day. It also provides room for inspired thought, especially needed during times of adversity when yesterday's solutions fall short in new realities.

The journey toward inspired thought often ends in a simple sense of joy and delight. The process is complex, however, beginning with two preconditions in the brain:

1. The presence of connected neural networks of information
2. The ability those networks have to adapt, to form and reform into new and novel connections (Johnson, 2010)

In his recent book, *The Brain and Emotional Intelligence: New Insights*, Daniel Goleman (2011) emphasizes the role of neural networks during creative thought, and their ability to adapt and connect. He says that EEGs of people during a creative moment show that the instant before answers come, the brain spikes with gamma activity (this spike, by the way, is what creates that little thrill you experience when you have an a-ha! moment). Goleman writes,

"Gamma activity indicates the binding together of neurons, as far-flung brain cells connect in a new neural network—as when a new association emerges. Immediately after that gamma spike, the new idea enters our consciousness" (Kindle Location 223).

Explore and Learn

Translated into practical action, the preconditions in the brain, required for inspired thought, imply that you must be a voracious learner and an adventurous experiencer of life. You have to go where what you know in your specialty area has a chance to bump up against ideas in fields other than your own; you have to live big (which may explain why most resilient leaders love the challenge of working for a greater good—it forces them into bigger risks and bigger experiences). In the classic book, *A Whack on the Side of the Head: How You Can Be More Creative*, Roger von Oech encourages those in search of creative problem solving to become explorers. Quoting journalist Robert Wieder, von Oech writes "Anyone can look for fashion in a boutique or history in a museum. The creative person looks for history in a hardware store and fashion in an airport" (p. 108).

Taking a cue from children, your road to renewal might also come from play or stimulations associated with the right brain, indulged in after hours, at retreats, on weekends, and on vacations where you escape from your usual routines (Pink, 2009). Travel, arts and crafts, metaphor, performing arts, music, tours of exhibits, playing with the dog, hiking, cooking, poetry, photography, storytelling—all of these are portals to renewal.

While renewal does not eliminate the demands of life and work, it does provide energy for individuals, teams, and systems to remain creative and relevant while meeting those demands. Renewal creates interludes; time where your brain can go right (instead of spinning in left brain) and think more creatively—even about complex problems.

If you still doubt that renewal is key to breakthrough thinking, test it yourself by noticing when inspired thought strikes you and what others tell you about when good ideas come to them. For example, I (Elle) just love the email sent to me by one of my education colleagues, Tracee Grigsby Turner, about a tricky data analysis project we were working on together. Her email said, "I had an insight last night in the hot tub, to look at a couple of cohort groups." It turned out Tracee's hot tub idea was a good one—when she drilled into the data, she discovered a positive trend in reading for two groups of students— data that provided hope and focus to a high school faculty that previously had neither.

On-the-Job Renewal

Just as engaging in your favorite activities outside the workday is critical to inspired thought, on-the-job interludes of renewal help you sustain your energy and ability to think creatively throughout the workday.

Given the importance of renewal to personal energy and innovation, it really is important and exciting to understand what organizations can do to promote and support renewal on the job. For years, I (Elle) have been writing about on-the-job sources of energy and renewal for leaders who are passionately engaged in meaningful work (Allison et al., 2012). In 2011, I began asking leaders to tell me what gives them happiness and energy on the job and during the workday. In this ongoing study, responses from leaders have rendered hundreds of data points that provide clues about the characteristics of systems that promote energy in people.

What might surprise and please you to learn is that what leaders find most energizing on the job has very little to do with escaping the demands of the organization, and more to do with experiencing relationships, problem solving, learning, expressing gratitude, and making a difference for others.

Sources of Workplace Energy and Joy

Figure 3.1 displays the on-the-job energy sources named by leaders most often when asked for their top three. As you can see, the leaders in this ongoing

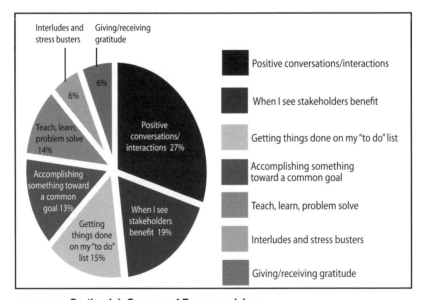

FIGURE 3.1 **On-the-Job Sources of Energy and Joy**

study report an increase in energy when they focus on meaningful work and meaningful relationships. Not surprising, given most nurse leaders' penchant for learning, many of the same sources of on-the-job energy are hallmarks of quality professional development and learning organizations (Senge, 1990).

Charlotte Fritz, who is an assistant professor in organizational psychology at Portland State University, also conducted research and discovered results related to mine. In an interview with Fritz that appeared in the May 2012 Harvard Business Review she says, "Taking short breaks during the workday doesn't revitalize you—unless you do something job related and positive such as praising a colleague or learning something new" (p. 34).

Ideas for On-the-Job Interludes That Also Sustain Your Focus on Work

Based on what brings people on-the-job joy and energy, combined with the prevailing assumption that workday focus is a source of renewal for resilient leadership, here are several examples of on-the-job interludes (Allison, 2011). What will you add to this list?

Lunch and Listen Part 1. Eat lunch with someone who will just listen (not give advice or tell you what to do) as you describe something you love about your work. Limit lunch to one hour. Stay focused; no gossip.

Lunch and Listen Part 2. Take an aspiring leader to lunch with the specific intent to just listen to them (not give advice or tell them what to do) as they describe what they think is possible in their work. Limit lunch to one hour. Stay focused; no gossip.

Find the Stories. Interview stakeholders, colleagues, and students about something your organization did for them. Take digital photos of each person and put them in a scrapbook along with a couple of quotes from the conversation. Later, when you need renewal and inspiration, thumb through the scrapbook and you will be reminded about how your work makes a difference. After you make the scrapbook, upload the photos into a digital photo frame where they constantly scroll and infuse the workplace with positive energy.

Walk and Learn. Walk down the hall and ask one or two people to tell you what they've learned today. Be sure to tell them that the reason you are asking this question is so you can feel renewed. This will make people more forthcoming because they want to be supportive of you.

My Favorite Mistake. Make a 10-minute renewal date with someone you work with. When you meet up, tell your coworker about your favorite mistake—something related to your meaningful work that might have gone wrong, but that taught you the most valuable lesson.

See Systemic Connections. Make a list of the decisions facing you over the next 12 months. Then make another list of the data (including surveys, focus groups, trend data, quarterly data) needed for each decision. Notice the overlap and rejoice over it. You see, complex decisions usually have systemic connections, so you can leverage information that helps with one decision to another decision.

Get Some Coaching. Schedule a coaching session with someone you work with who has great coaching skills and will ask you the kind of thought leadership questions that create breakthroughs in your thinking. Send them a thank you card afterward with an invitation to reciprocate. Senior leaders who coach their colleagues and direct reports learn more about the work of others and gain insight into the whole system.

Thanks for the Opportunity. Write a thank you note to someone for something they allowed you to do to make the organization better. Deliver it to them in person if you can. They may be perplexed at first: "What? You're thanking me for something you did?" Tell them you are thanking them because they gave you the chance to lead and grow.

Thanks in Advance. Write a thank-you note in advance to someone expressing your gratitude in advance for something you need from them. You'll learn how to ask for what you need, and you'll experience gratitude, which is a source of renewal and energy. The other person gains the experience of giving and supporting a colleague.

Have a Research Date. Pick up one of your go-to professional journals that you never get to read and skim the table of contents, looking for something that sparks your curiosity. Make one copy of the article, bring it to a colleague, and ask him or her to meet you for lunch or a break where you can read it together and talk about it. Your colleague gets to pick the article the next time.

Make an Artistic Display of Data. Review key indicators for a project you are leading. Get a poster sheet and markers and represent the data in a format you've never considered before. Or, go to a website such as that of easel.ly (http://www.easel.ly/) that allows you to make infographics for free. Explain your data display with your team.

If you try some of these ideas, I'd love to hear how they worked for you. Send me an e-mail at elle@wisdomout.com.

When your brief on-the-job interludes sustain your focus on work, you accomplish more during the workday. This, combined with longer episodes of renewal and rejuvenation outside of the workday—going to the zoo, taking vacations, not working on most weekends—create positive conditions for resilient leadership; not only will you have more energy to accomplish meaningful work, but you will experience greater creativity that leads to insight and you will accomplish more during the workday—which gives you more time off for renewal outside of work. Talk about a win-win-win proposition.

Let's Talk About Lunch

In addition to short, work-related interludes, nurses and nurse leaders also need food and water breaks! In fact, as some hospitals have found, lunch breaks can be an essential strategy for Transforming Care at the Bedside (TCAB) initiatives. For some nurses, who are trying to increase the amount of time they spend at the bedside, taking lunch breaks is counterintuitive. But, as they found at Massachusetts General Hospital, one-hour lunch breaks allowed nurses to return to their patients refreshed and renewed. The breaks also promoted greater teamwork between nurses as they pitched in to help each other in order to make getting to lunch more likely and less stressful.

Cultivating Renewal to Enable Resilience

Leaders who engage in renewal outside of work and in short interludes during the workday increase their leadership resilience. Not only do they enjoy enhanced physical and emotional health, but they also increase their ability to manage their emotions, think well, and meet the demands of the day. Difficult though it may be, resilient leaders choose to make lifestyle choices that promote their health and prolong their lives. These choices not only make you a more resilient leader, but they also enhance your well-being and they simply make life more delightful and work more satisfying.

The Greater Good: The Deepest Well

Hands down, the deepest source of renewal for resilient leaders comes from doing work that matters—work for a greater good. Reciprocally, the energy that comes from doing meaningful work enables resilient leaders to accomplish even more meaningful work. The greater good gives meaning to the struggle. As one leader put it, "For me renewal comes from knowing that I make a difference and that I'm doing the right things. Knowing that I do the right things gives me strength to show up every day and do more right things."

Referring to the greater good as "something bigger," Leider and Shapiro write:

> *What is important is that we have a sense of place regarding the sources of our conception of the good life. While the manner in which we express ourselves is going to be highly individual, the central core of what we aspire to needs, it seems, to be grounded in something other than our own individual aspirations. We make the meaning of our lives, in other words, but that meaning apparently depends on something outside them. (2002, p. 39)*

Guided by her deep religious convictions, nurse leader Connie Hill finds renewal in creating sustainable solutions to benefit the most vulnerable populations. For example, when she was a unit director at Children's Memorial Hospital in Chicago, Connie learned that a lack of community resources prevented a child on a ventilator from being released from the hospital. Her response was to form a consortium of advocates and service providers to support this child and to work together on behalf of all children with special needs. Connie says, "I become energized when I find answers to problems that others say cannot be solved."

Currently, as a nurse and as a nurse educator in the San Francisco Bay Area, Connie continues to make a difference at the community level helping what she calls "the underserved and the disconnected." Although Connie could have focused her doctoral research in any number of clinical areas, she chose to concentrate on the lives of emerging young adults born with HIV. Using PhotoVoice, a process for both documenting and illuminating social issues, Connie said, "I wanted to see through their eyes, how these teens live; how they experience life, and who they are collectively. I want to help them share their story." Newly married to a pastor in the high-poverty community of Richmond California, Connie has started a non-profit organization to bring resources such as healthy food to the community. Connie says, "I know it might sound crazy, but doing this extra work in the community gives me energy for my work in nursing. This is what feeds me, this is what makes me resilient."

What Makes a Greater Good?

The greater good is not an abstract principle even if at first it may be challenging to comprehend. Put simply, the greater good is a conscious creation of results that produce benefits that transcend the needs of any one person or group to benefit more people and groups, especially the most vulnerable, and for the long term (Allison et al., 2012).

In many ways, the Triple Aim is an example of the greater good in action within the healthcare community. As its name suggests, the Triple Aim is a challenge to nursing to achieve three related outcomes:

1. To increase the healthcare quality for patients
2. To improve population health
3. To reduce healthcare costs (Stiefel and Nolan, 2012)

The three-prong purpose of the Triple Aim elevates it from a one-dimensional strategy to reduce healthcare costs alone, at the expense of the most vulnerable populations. It challenges us to work at local levels to improve the health of communities through a sustainable focus on wellness education, while reducing costs. Responses to the Triple Aim Challenge will require an agile ability on the part of nursing staffs to test multiple hunches simultaneously in order to discover what works. Resilient nursing staffs will embrace the challenge and will likely find themselves energized by the difference they make for their patients and communities.

Most nurse leaders find that the qualities that signal a greater good are also rewarding in their own right. They stimulate emotions of compassion and gratitude, both of which are known to elicit a sense of well-being. How would producing the following qualities of the greater good also bring renewal to you?

- The greater good is inclusive: It seeks to create benefits for all community members.
- The greater good seeks to create important, needed, and meaningful change.
- The greater good is a by-product of many people tackling complex, persistent, and vexing problems from different angles.
- The greater good seeks insight from problems rather than just containing them.
- The greater good considers the impact on future generations for the long term and builds in safeguards to minimize unintentional consequences.
- The greater good is made visible through action taken by those who see the need for change.
- The greater good is brought about by individuals seeking real accomplishment and humbly accepting accolades as by-products of meaningful work.
- The greater good arises out of processes that align with the outcomes; the end does not justify the means.
- The greater good is coherent to the mission and highest purpose of the organization.
- The greater good creates and opens up leadership opportunities for others.
- The greater good simultaneously transforms the culture surrounding the initiative in order to create partnerships that empower people to renew and therefore sustain the initiative.
- The greater good is often fueled by personal passion that begs to manifest through the leader's role.

Deal with Busyness

At this point, you might be thinking "All this talk of the greater good is well and fine, but we're already working hard and people are exhausted and stressed out. We're just too busy to do anything more." Webster's New World Dictionary defines busy as "used up, not available, as with a telephone." Not a glamorous definition of leadership by anyone's terms, yet many leaders spend inordinate amounts of time telling others just how busy they are. An unrelenting sense of busyness is a sure signal that you are spending more time putting out fires and being distracted by short-term tasks, and less time engaged in meaningful work. As if all that were not bad enough, busyness is also one of the most pervasive sources of stress.

Busyness often signals a lack of focus. Leaders who lose their battle with busyness are so overwhelmed with daily demands and putting out fires that they do not have energy, let alone time, for aspirational work. What to do about busyness? Ironically, there is nothing like a new and meaningful project to cure a leader of busyness and focus their time and energy. Although it will feel counterintuitive to busy leaders, you do yourself a service when you get going on a complex project that matters to you and that serves your organization. When you do, you will have no other choice but to reprioritize less important obligations and needs.

Manage Your Stress: A Dreadful Robber of Energy and Happiness

Like air hunger in the context of leadership, the need for renewal comes not so much from a lack of free time, coffee breaks, and vacations, as it does from the presence of multiple, myriad stresses that threaten to overwhelm us. Renewal, in all of its various forms, is the antidote to leadership stress. While engaging in meaningful work may be the greatest source of renewal for resilient nurse leaders, unmanaged and unrelenting stress efficiently undermines it. New understandings about the science behind stress strongly recommend that renewal for stress reduction become a priority in all of our lives.

Telomeres

To get the conversation started, let us consider the miraculous placement of telomeres in your cells. First a definition: Telomeres are stubs of DNA that protect the ends of your chromosomes (Epel et al., 2004; de Lange, Lundblad, & Blackburn, 2006). I (Elle) picture telomeres as duct tape, wrapped around the frayed ends of electrical cords. Blackburn (2009) likens them to aglets, the plastic caps found on the tips of a good pair of shoelaces. Whichever metaphor works for you, you can imagine either one—duct tape or shoelace tips—breaking down over time. In fact, every time your cells replicate, small amounts of your telomeres naturally wear away in the process—just like duct tape and aglets do when they are regularly handled. Eventually the telomeres and the DNA they contain on the chromosomes at the ends of your cells wear away entirely, and the cell naturally dies (Zolli & Healy, 2012). Not to be morbid, but over time, more and more of your cells naturally die. Eventually and inevitably, so do you.

While you seemingly have no control over the natural aging process, you do have some control over stress, which, in addition to normal cell division, is another source of wear and tear on telomeres and is an accelerant of the aging process. Stress ages us during the biological process most of us know as the fight or flight response, when adrenaline and norepinephrine pump into your body. This is bad news because it turns out that excess quantities of stress hormones such as adrenaline and norepinephrine also erode your telomeres. To make matters worse, psychological stress can keep you in a steady state of fight or flight, literally bathing your telomeres with potent mixtures of stress hormones that accelerate their degradation (Epel et al., 2004; Goleman, 2011; Sapolsky, 2004).

Now for some good news. An enzyme called telomerase, when present in relevant amounts (which can be detected and measured through blood tests), mitigates the effects of natural aging and stress on your telomeres. And here is the really good news: You can increase telomerase in your body by engaging in activities that reduce stress (Blackburn, 2009; Epel et al., 2004; Goleman, 2011; Sapolsky, 2004). You just have to choose to do so.

Ways to Mitigate the Effects of Stress

Writing about the mitigating effects of meditation on stress, Zolli and Healy quote researchers Jacobs and Saron who conclude

> *Activities that increase a person's sense of well-being may have a profound effect on the most fundamental aspects of their physiology. It doesn't necessarily have to be meditation per se; it's really about creating conditions in which you can flourish and your purpose can come into being. (2012, p. 140)*

Although increased well-being and a corresponding increase in your body's production of telomerase can be achieved in a variety of ways, several strategies come to the forefront for their powerful ability to alleviate stress and increase the lifespan of your telomeres (Epel et al., 2004; Sapolsky, 2004):

- **Physical exercise.** According to studies conducted by Elizabeth Blackburn at the University of California, San Francisco, exercise is one of the best strategies for mitigating the effects of stress hormones on your telomeres (O'Brien, 2011). If you are not physically active, the best thing you can do for the students and communities you serve is to get active now. If you are already active, don't stop, especially when you feel overwhelmed. The impact of a sedentary lifestyle is so pronounced that Harvard Business Review blogger Nilofer Merchant (2013) announced, "sitting is the smoking of our generation."

- **Sleep.** New research from the University of California, Berkeley, shows that lack of sleep makes you more than tired and irritable; it also may increase your level of generalized anxiety. Sleep deprivation makes you anxious because it causes other parts of your brain, specifically the amygdala and insular cortex, to go on high alert, producing the kind of anxiety associated with excessive worrying (Goldstein et al., 2013). When excessive worrying from lack of sleep becomes chronic, it is as if you are in a constant state of fight or flight, a condition that increases stress hormone production.

- **Affinity groups.** Join a support group or offer to mentor or coach someone else. Researchers Elizabeth Blackburn and Elissa Epel (2009) looked at the benefits of belonging to affinity groups for mothers caring for severely handicapped children and conclude that when it comes to mitigating the deadly effects of stress, belonging to a support group can make a difference—but not primarily for the reason you think. It turns out that belonging to a support group allows you to feel compassion, and the compassion one feels when supporting another person appears to stimulate the production of telomerase. In other words, the compassion you feel when you belong to a group of people who are struggling with issues similar to you also mitigates stress for yourself at a cellular level. Compassion feels good.

- **Reframe your perspective.** Every day, large and small stressors challenge even the most optimistic among us. Stress researchers say that when events stress us out, it is often because we feel we have no control over them. True, there are many things in life we cannot control. For everything else, we can choose to reframe the way we look at it (Seligman, 2011a; Singer, 2011).

- **Meditation and mindfulness training.** People who are meditation practitioners will tell you that one of the greatest gifts it offers is not learning how to empty one's mind of thought but learning to become more mindful. Meditation, which is the ability to observe and experience one's thoughts and one's experiences without reacting and without exhibiting emotional upset (Zolli & Healy, 2012), is a powerful antidote to the feelings of disorientation that come with adversity and disruptive change (See Chapter 6 for a simple exercise to increase mindfulness).

Summary

In this chapter, we explored the importance of renewal to leadership resilience. Renewal bolsters your leadership resilience; it creates energy for you to show up for your life and your work, and it enables you to bounce forward in times of adversity and disruptive change. Renewal helps sustain a healthy mind and body, but it also makes you think better. Interludes of renewal both on the job and off the clock are essential for resilient leadership. Stress and busyness are dreadful robbers of happiness—and therefore, of resilience—and they prevent leaders from getting to meaningful work for the greater good. The good news is that leaders can take steps to mitigate stress and deal with busyness.

Activities and Questions

1. Go to www.anahra.org to participate in the ANA-sponsored comprehensive health risk appraisal (HRA) in collaboration with Pfizer Inc., free of charge. This HIPAA-compliant appraisal will provide you with real-time data on your personal and professional health, safety, and wellness. You will also have the opportunity to compare your results to national averages and ideal standards. Upon completion of the HRA, nurses are directed to a web wellness portal, filled with interactive quizzes, games, and pertinent resources.

2. The following list of activities and questions was first published on the Wisdom Out website (Allison-Napolitano, 2011b):

   - Exercise! (Feed your telomeres). Watch this YouTube video on telomeres: https://www.youtube.com/watch?v=9o1HIuI6Z8k

   - Smile and laugh. Watch this TED Talk by Ron Gutman on the hidden power of smiling: https://www.ted.com/talks/ron_gutman_the_hidden_power_of_smiling

   - To help eliminate a sense of busyness, make a list of 10 things that would take you 15 minutes or less to complete. Before you go to bed each night, do one to three of the items and cross them off your list.

- Establish a transition activity at the end of the day from work to home. Share your strategy with your colleagues. For example, one leader said that as soon as he hits the freeway which is about one mile from his office, he stops ruminating about work and purposefully thinks about home, family, and his hobbies.

- Ask for a 20 minute peer coaching session so you can think through something that matters to the meaningful work you do.

- Don't sacrifice good for the illusion of perfection. (We spend a lot of energy making small things perfect—which is a form of procrastination.)

- Go to bed 15 minutes earlier.

- Go for a midday walk.

- Turn off the "ding" sound on your cell phone and computer.

- Refuse to use your cell phone when you drive.

- Mindfully choose to let something urgent but unimportant go. In a short while, it will no longer be urgent and may prove to be irrelevant too. Reflect on the results of this choice.

4

Resonance
Great Leaders Move Us

—Annie McKee and Richard Boyatzis, authors of *Resonant Leadership*

A good way to begin to understand the power of resonance is to think about a person you know who is really great to be around—someone who positively changes the atmosphere in the room when they walk in the door and who creates a good vibe. Perhaps you are thinking of a parent or sibling who gave you confidence to pursue your education and career. Or, perhaps the person you are thinking of was or currently is your boss and he or she has a way of listening to your ideas and letting you talk them through. Maybe you are thinking of a co-worker whose sense of humor makes work a joy and brings out the best in everyone on your shift.

Now, switch gears a bit and think about your work and life accomplishments that you attribute to the inspiration and energy you receive from interacting with this person. You see, leadership resonance is the ability to create a positive emotional force field that has a way of moving other people to action—and action is the crux of leadership resilience.

Sharon Rohrbach is one of those nurse leaders with a knack for moving people to action in the face of harsh adversity. Over the years as a neonatal nurse, Sharon saw too many babies return to the hospital emergency room within days of going home after they were born, often dying of causes that could have been prevented. She realized that the mothers of these infants were vulnerable themselves, living in poverty or without a support system or using drugs or alcohol. They did not recognize the signs of fever, feeding problems, or other factors that signaled their infant's distress. After she watched one baby die in his mother's arms, Sharon decided to do something about it. At first Sharon attributed the problem to the insurance companies and their policies to send mothers home within 24 hours after giving birth. But, as she told me (Elle) in 2012, "That was a dead end I did not pursue. In fact we realized we needed to do a lot more than get the insurance companies to increase the time these new mothers and babies could stay in the hospital." As a result, Sharon founded Nurses for Newborns, a non-profit organization in Tennessee and Missouri that sends a nurse home with new mothers who need support, and who need to be shown how to care for their babies.

Debbie Layton was the first nurse Sharon hired for Nurses for Newborns, back in 1991. Debbie says, "I was working as a nurse in the hospital and raising young kids and I needed another job to round things out. I came upon a flyer Sharon had posted about needing nurses for her company and I gave her a call. She was thunderstruck to hear from me, but even from the flyer, I could tell that the work she was doing was important. I wanted to be a part of it."

Great Leaders Move Us

Sharon Rorhbach possesses a megadose of what we've come to know as emotional resonance, which is also an essential enabler of leadership resilience. The more you have cultivated the ability to interact with people from an emotionally resonant stance, the more practiced and empowered you are to do so during times of adversity. Resonance ignites people with hope, optimism, and commitment, and provides leaders with an uncommon knack for rallying the organization during times of disruptive change. Resonant leaders have a way of putting people at ease, even in difficult situations. They infuse people with hope and possibility, and somehow they inspire people to interact from their best selves. As a result, they motivate individuals and teams to tackle difficult issues and come up with solutions that serve a greater good.

In the foreword of Boyatzis and McKee's book *Resonant Leadership: Renewing Yourself and Connecting With Others Through Mindfulness, Hope, and Compassion* (2005), Daniel Goleman explains that emotionally resonant leaders are those who are self-aware, socially aware, and self-motivated. Goleman writes that these individuals are "able to somehow radiate that positivity, igniting and mobilizing positive attitudes in those around them." To understand the practical application of resonance you only have to recall those times when you've said about someone, "I like her vibe!" or "I love working with him; he has good energy," or "She has great mojo and always gets things done—of course I'll help her out." As Deb Layton says about Sharon Rorhbach, "It is the way Sharon delivers her message. She is very calm, positive and has a loving demeanor. The more you work with her, the more you want to do this work." These comments are markers for resonance; they signal the favorable emotional energy you detect in those who compel you to action.

The Resonance Inventory

Before reading on, take a few moments to respond to the Resonance Inventory (to take the online version, please visit www.WisdomOut.com) depicted in Exercise 4.1, which will provide you with objective feedback about your current state of resonance.

Instructions: Respond to each of the following statements quickly, providing your first impulse as the answer. If you are responding as a team, look at the average response or look at the amount of responses for each number in the range. A response of 10 is the strongest possible agreement, and 1 is the strongest possible disagreement. There are no correct answers.

Exercise 4.1 Resonance Inventory

Statement	Strongly Disagree									Strongly Agree
1. When I see colleagues I didn't know well or a complete stranger crying, it makes me uncomfortable. The last thing I want to know is the details of another person's life. They may have problems, but they certainly do not involve me.	1	2	3	4	5	6	7	8	9	10
2. Whenever I see a group of people laughing, it makes me worry that either I didn't get the joke or perhaps that they are secretly laughing at me. I never join in the laughter, but either avoid the situation entirely or suggest that we've got serious work to do and we had better get to it.	1	2	3	4	5	6	7	8	9	10
3. When I notice a friend, family member, or colleague who is clearly fearful, I try to help them snap out of it.—"Hey," I tell them, "you're not a kid, and there are no dragons under the bed anymore!" If they pull this fear act too often, I tell them to grow up and start acting their age. In fact, it's unsettling to me when people around me show fear.	1	2	3	4	5	6	7	8	9	10
4. When I see someone taking pride in something minuscule—like thinking that their grandkid is the only cute baby in the world—I just tune it out. "Okay. Your kid's on the honor roll and is really, really gifted—and so are you. So can we get back to work now?"	1	2	3	4	5	6	7	8	9	10
5. When colleagues or friends are perpetually happy, it makes me wonder about them. These are serious times, and serious people don't get into good moods unless they are in active denial. They must not watch the news, and they certainly don't know what's going on in our organization, or they would be a bit more sober and take life more seriously. Their good moods make me question their judgment and grip on reality.	1	2	3	4	5	6	7	8	9	10

6. I secretly admire some leaders whom other people seem to despise. They are tough but I think they are fair. When they chew somebody out publicly, they say out loud what I think—and what everybody thinks but just won't say.	1	2	3	4	5	6	7	8	9	10
7. My siblings, family, and close friends know not to intrude too much on my personal feelings. They know I don't appreciate anybody else, no matter how close they may be, asking me how I feel about things.	1	2	3	4	5	6	7	8	9	10
8. If a colleague gives a presentation and starts to choke up at the end when he or she talks about how important the topic is to him or her or to the organization, I find it embarrassing and totally unprofessional.	1	2	3	4	5	6	7	8	9	10
9. If I see a colleague or friend get too emotional, I try to help them out by lightening up the mood and changing the subject.	1	2	3	4	5	6	7	8	9	10
10. It hardly ever happens, but on those very rare occasions when my emotions get the better of me, I just excuse myself. I'd much rather be alone than around family, friends, or colleagues when I'm emotional.	1	2	3	4	5	6	7	8	9	10

Total Score: _____

Reflection on Your Score

Take a moment to reflect on the results of your Resonance Inventory.

My Resonance Inventory Score is: _____

Highlight key insights from the score interpretation you received. What sounds right to you? What seems off? What goals do you want to set for yourself or for your team?

Interpreting Your Score

Where do highly resilient people tend to score on the Resonance Inventory? Leaders who take the online version of the Resonance Inventory, and who also rate themselves high on happiness and meaningful work, score most often in the range of 10–40.

If You Score in the Range of 10–40: Although at times it seems that you wear your heart on your sleeve, you usually have the ability to frame your strong emotions and the emotions of others in ways that people around you perceive as helpful, empathetic, and compassionate. You likely have a strong ability to set an emotional tone for the organization that helps people move forward. For example, when grieving would help, you are not too embarrassed or too shy to display sadness. When inspired action and creativity are needed, you are the first one to display hope and excitement. You have a knack for contextualizing your emotions in the mission and vision of the group in ways that others find credible and authentic. Your social-emotional awareness makes you a helpful coach for your colleagues and peers. Usually, you are able to maintain your equanimity in the company of those in distress without being taken advantage of by someone who uses emotional displays for the purpose of manipulation. The challenge for you when it comes to emotional intelligence is remaining productive and focused toward movement when your emotions or the emotions of others could take you off track. On occasion, you might also need to buffer yourself better from the effect of others' emotions on you.

If You Score in the Range of 41–70: Although you are aware of your emotions and how they affect others, you may appear to others to be too calculating in the emotions you decide to share with others and the emotions you decide to keep in check. While your ability to monitor and regulate your emotions is usually helpful, you may come across to others as being inauthentic in your emotional response. As a result, you may not be using your own emotional reality to inspire others to action. You can get better at this by contextualizing your emotions within the mission and vision of the team or organization.

Show and tell others what you feel and how it connects to meaningful work. Do the same for others too. When the people around you display strong emotions, help them reframe them as calls to action and resilience.

If You Score in the Range of 71–100: It's almost always good to be rational—and you certainly are. It's sometimes good to be alone—and you probably are. But it's not helpful to be angry, sullen, cynical, distrustful, vengeful, spiteful, and full of regret. It may feel to you that the people around you are attempting to take advantage of you, manipulate you, and prey on your feelings. At times, however, it might occur to you that rationality alone is not the key to happiness. After all, lots of people know that the square of the hypotenuse is equal to the sum of the square of the two sides, and they are right. But being right is not always enough—you also need to connect with people at an emotional level.

A Force Field of Positive Energy

Resonance is a force field of positive energy projected outward from one person, infusing those around them with hope, vision, and compassion (Boyatzis & McKee, 2005). Resonance also has a ripple effect; the positive emotions embedded in resonance are contagious, and the resonance of a single leader can set the tone for the entire organization. When adversity and disruptive change strikes, resilient leaders are never more resonant. They maintain their presence and keep their cool even when chaos swirls about them.

As with the other inventories provided to you in this book, the online version of the Resonance Inventory (that you completed in the exercise above) first asks participants to rate their level of happiness about their work and the extent to which they believe their work is meaningful to the organization. What I (Elle) have found from analyzing the data is that the leaders who rate themselves high on both happiness and meaningful work fall in a range of resonance that reveals a high level of emotional interaction with others. This range certainly is in opposition to the category at the other end of the scale where emotions are shunned in favor of rational hard data, but it is even left of the center range, where emotions and rationality are more balanced.

Leaders who score on the more emotional side of the scale emphasize the need to reign in their own emotions, especially those that are negative or overzealous, while they simultaneously accept and show compassion for the emotions of others. This mixture of self-awareness and openness to others is what it takes to keep people moving forward.

The key to harnessing strong emotions without becoming overwhelmed is in learning how to contextualize them—how to place them in the stories of specific patients, families, and other stakeholders and relate them to the mission of the organization. Commenting on the research of neuroscientist Richard Davidson, who looks at different emotional styles that originate in the brain, Daniel Goleman implies that people who experience deeper emotions may even have an advantage over those who are less emotional, provided they find a way to communicate them: "Some people experience their feelings quite intensely, some people quite shallowly. Those who have stronger feelings may be better able to authentically communicate them more powerfully—to move people" (2011, Kindle Location 365–367).

Here is a story to illustrate this point: Bianca is a new nurse leader with strong feelings about decentralizing hospital nursing teams to put them closer to the patients. When Bianca passionately led a task force to champion the new initiative, she met with a great deal of resistance from a number of nurses on the unit who enjoyed the camaraderie that came with working from a centralized station and who interpreted her enthusiasm for change as criticism for their performance. In an unsuccessful effort to persuade the nurses to try the decentralized approach, Bianca explained to them that they would use smart phones and other strategies to connect and collaborate with each other as needed. This was not a selling point! Many of the more veteran nurses were not crazy about using the new technologies and felt even more resistant to Bianca's leadership.

The turning point came for Bianca when she focused on the experience of the patients and improved outcomes shown in other decentralized models—outcomes that appealed to the nurses in her unit and helped them see how decentralized nursing stations could support other important goals. It was only after Bianca connected her strong emotions about decentralized nurse teams to the larger and shared goals of the organization that the nurses on her unit began to see why they needed to be more open to the concept.

Stories are a great way to contextualize emotions and link them to compelling futures. Especially during challenges, stories help people make sense of disorder and begin to shape new realities. Bern Melnyk, who is Dean, Associate Vice President for Health Promotion, and Chief Wellness Officer at Ohio State University says, "I am a big storyteller, and I am more than willing to tell stories about my own life. My stories help people understand who I am and where I am coming from."

In his book about how the stories we tell ourselves shape the lives we lead (and how the lives we lead are a result of the stories we tell ourselves), Jim Loehr (2007) writes "True success is realizable when one consciously crafts an ambitious, achievable story and then sticks to it" (p. 48). Loehr's point is that stories can create the outcomes we desire. Although Sharon Rorhbach of Nurses for Newborns is a leader who expertly collects and uses data, she too believes that stories are a great way to appeal emotionally to people and motivate them to action. Sharon says, "People don't get as excited by numbers as they do by stories. Stories help people see how they can make a difference."

How Resonance Enables Resilience

Resonance is achieved when leaders positively drive the emotions of the workforce, inspiring it to accomplish the good work of the organization even in the face of continual change and downright adversity. Dissonance, on the other hand, results when emotional securities are undermined and people become less able to accomplish goals (Goleman, Boyatzis, & McKee, 2004). The more resonant you are as a leader, the more able you are to move others forward in the aftermath of change. In the words of Boyatzis and McKee (2005), authors on resonant leadership topics, "Great leaders move us" (p. 1).

Emotional Intelligence and Emotional Brain Patterns

Resonance largely depends on your *emotional intelligence* (EI)—especially your ability to manage your emotions and set the emotional tone for others. Goleman, who was trained as a psychologist at Harvard and was also a science writer for the New York Times, was the first person to bring emotional intelligence to the attention of contemporary audiences. Goleman frames his theory of emotional intelligence in the workplace, and he particularly elaborates on emotional intelligence as applied to leaders (1998, 2004). Goleman's EI model is made up of four domains: self-awareness, self-management, social awareness, and relationship management. Each domain is comprised of several competencies, some that have to do with being aware of emotions and how they are operating on people and the organization, and others that have to do with taking action to regulate those emotions for the good of themselves, others, and the organization (1998).

Emotional Styles

New research from neuroscientist Richard Davidson provides additional insight into emotional intelligence. In his book *The Emotional Life of Your Brain: How Its Unique Patterns Affect the Way You Think, Feel and Live— and How You*

A Brief Summary of the Four Domains of Emotional Intelligence

- Domain 1: Self-Awareness

  Leaders who are good in self-awareness can read their own emotions and recognize their impact on others. They also are aware of their own strengths and limits, and possess a solid sense of self-worth.

- Domain 2: Self-Management

  Leaders who are good in self-management keep their emotions in check, respond well to changing situations, have a personal drive to improve, take action when presented with opportunities, and are optimistic in their views.

- Domain 3: Social Awareness

  Leaders who are strong in social awareness notice the emotions of others and are sensitive to them. They also detect how emotions play out in the climate of the organization. They are politically astute and seek to meet the needs of others.

- Domain 4: Relationship Management

  Finally, leaders who are strong in relationship management use a compelling vision to inspire others and have a variety of strategies (such as coaching) to influence and develop people and teams. These leaders are skilled at leading change and at creating relationships that create solid backing for organizational change.

Can Change Them (2012), Davidson explains that his research arose out of two observations: first, that different people respond differently to life's trials, and second that the people he knows who go through life with equanimity all do something quite deliberate and mindful, like meditation, for example, to have that ability. In other words, these individuals were not emotionally balanced all the time, but they became that way by taking advantage of neuroplasticity and providing themselves with experiences that reshaped the circuitry in their brain.

These two observations led Davidson to focus his research first on how the structure and neuroactivity of the brain creates different emotional styles in different people. Second, Davidson showed how practices that promote well-being (such as meditation) operate on the mind, which over time restructures the brain—in this case, toward a style of functioning that is more level-headed, calm, and composed in the face of disruption. In his book, Davidson describes six emotional styles that people possess in combination, to various degrees:

1. **Resilience.** How rapidly or slowly you recover from adversity.
2. **Outlook.** How long positive emotions persist following a joyful event.
3. **Social Intuition.** The accuracy with which you detect nonverbal social cues from others.
4. **Context.** The extent to which you regulate your emotions according to the context.
5. **Self-Awareness.** Your awareness of your own bodily signals that constitute emotion.
6. **Attention.** The extent to which your attention is either focused or scattered.

Some people pick up on their emotions and the emotions of others very well and are relatively unflappable and recover quickly from distress. These individuals are more able to detect growing emotional dissonance in themselves and others and take steps to turn things around. Others are easily upset and take a long time to recover and seem to be unaware of emotional changes in themselves and others. Referencing Davidson's work, Goleman observes that the latter group also tends to be chronic worriers, thereby putting themselves in a state of continual emotional hijacking that generates stress and produces stress hormones that wreak havoc on emotional and physiological well-being. Goleman says, "Given the many realistic stresses we face, those first two styles—being unflappable and capable of quick recovery—are the most effective in navigating the troubles of the world of work" (2011, Kindle Location 363–364).

On the topic of picking up on the emotions of others, Megan Damon (nurse leader from Minnesota) points out that all nurse leaders have to remember they already possess heightened skills in emotional awareness that comes from their interactions with patients—they just have to remember to use them in their leadership role. She says:

> As bedside nurses, we had to quickly gain skills in developing rapport with patients. We had to pick up on facial expressions and notice things like if their hair was washed or not and what that might tell us about what is going on with them—we had to use our 'presence' to get into that emotional space.

Leaders need to tune in to their employees in much the same way. Megan says,

> *Our nurses expect us to know what is going on with them, to pick up subtle changes in patterns—simple things like, are they buying lunch when they used to bring it from home? Could this mean they are more stressed out?*

The point is not to intrusively inquire into every aspect of a colleague's life, but to engage with them in the present moment, and to help calibrate the emotional feeling of the workspace so that everyone can do their best work.

The Responsibility to Become More Resonant

Setting a resonant tone is not easy work. But resonant leaders must sustain their resonance even when—especially when—people around them are pessimistic or even hostile. For example, some nurse leaders who feel torn between advocating for their staff and being a management team player sometimes feel friendless on all sides. Nurse leader Nan Ybarra from Texas says it can be difficult to make the transition from the bedside to leadership. "All of a sudden I felt compartmentalized," she said. "I felt like I had to wear a bell like a cat so people could hear me coming." Reflecting on the isolation new nurse leaders can experience on the job, Tanya Osborne-McKenzie, a nurse leader in California remembers one of her assistants telling her, "Tanya, I am not like you, I *want* people to like me!" Tanya says, "Sure, nurse leaders have to deal with a lot of big things, but I've watched some nurse leaders become worn down by the day-to-day issues—including people who just don't like them simply because they are managers—that wear you down."

Challenging as it might be, leaders have a responsibility to increase their resonance for the simple fact that it makes others more resilient by increasing their health and adding to their lifespan. To illustrate, consider the research of Dr. Robert Sapolsky, whose study of the effects of hierarchical stress in primates (such as when the top male primate in the group pummels lower members of the group) offers pertinent insight for humans functioning in hierarchical organizations: The more stress placed on individuals from those above them in the hierarchy, the greater the chance they will become ill (Sapolsky, 2004).

Other related research out of Cal State focuses on the phenomenon of emotional contagion whereby leaders seemingly infect the people who work for them with their prevailing mood (Sy, Cote, & Saavedra, 2005). These researchers contrived an experiment where volunteers were told they would be participating in a team building exercise, and then were placed with a group leader who had either been exposed to "Saturday Night Live" skits (to create a positive mood) or a vignette on torture (to create a negative mood). They measured the moods of all the volunteers both before and after they worked through the team building task. As suspected, participants who were with positive mood leaders also had positive moods and participants with negative mood leaders were less positive.

In another study on leadership behavior and the effect it has on resilience in subordinates, researchers at the University of Nebraska found that participants who exhibited greater resilience mentioned their leaders as a positive factor over participants who were less resilient (Harland, Harrison, Jones, & Reiter Palmon, 2005).

Beyond the research, common sense tells us that leaders who yell at people, are impatient, withhold recognition, and don't include people in decisions that will affect them, create dissonant environments that literally make people sick. Bottom line, all leaders need to ask themselves these questions: Am I being intentional about the emotional force field I wish to create in my organization? Will the way I am managing my own emotions help to create this?

The Challenge for Novice Leaders

The responsibility to become more resonant is especially required for new or novice leaders who are inexperienced in setting the emotional tone for an entire organization or team and who have not learned to quell the cocky needs of their ego. Robert Sutton makes this point in a post he wrote for the online Bloomberg-Businessweek Magazine (2008). Sutton, a Stanford University professor and author of the book *The No Asshole Rule*, tells of an amusing study conducted by researchers at UC Berkeley who found that given the opportunity, people with new leadership powers will "eat more cookies, chew with their mouths open and leave more crumbs." One inference we can make from the "cookie study" is that because they lack the vast array of leadership experiences that would cultivate emotional connections in their brains, and/or because they lack awareness for how their behavior affects others, new leaders may be low in a number of the emotional styles Davidson writes about, especially social intuition, context, and self-awareness.

The impressions that others form about you during times of adversity also play a role in your career trajectory. When nurse leader and educator Enna Trevathan from the University of San Francisco was a young nurse, she recalls one night working in oncology when she became aware that a patient was in crisis. Enna says,

> *Something in my mind understood that everything was going south for this*
> *patient. I went in to see her and found blood all over the sheets. Here I am*
> *a brand new nurse, and all of a sudden I'm ordering transfusions. On top of*
> *it all, there were two patients I had not visited yet. I started to think of the*
> *smallness of me. At first I was upset with the nurse manager who put me in*
> *this position. But later, when I was asked to be team leader, she told me she*
> *watched me handle the situation well. She told me 'you need to be aware that*
> *you are always being tested.' After this experience, I began to see that I am*
> *stronger than I thought I was.*

Given that we now understand the contagious nature of emotions, and have ideas from neuroscientists about how we can reshape our brain patterns in order to behave with greater equanimity, only the most clueless of leaders would choose not to become more resonant.

Cultivating Resonance

The very real demands of leadership take their toll, making leaders less resonant or even dissonant in their interactions with others. Over time, a lack of positive resonance creates tension and distress in the organization. In a healthy economy where people have choices about where they work, persistent negative emotions—especially when the leader is the source of negativity— will drive people away. A fleeing workforce and the accompanying need to constantly recruit and train new employees undermines your ability to lead with resilience and undermines the resilience of the entire organization. In this section, you'll find several tactics for cultivating resonance—for making you more compassionate, hopeful, and mindful—and for transmitting those qualities throughout the organization.

Learn to Listen

Compassion is the act of understanding what people need and then feeling moved to take helpful and appropriate action on their behalf. During times of change, for example, leaders show compassion when they first take time to understand what their nurses need to implement new procedures and learn new skills. Compassion is impossible, however, if you are not a good listener. Leaders who have not learned how to effectively listen give the impression that they do not care, even when they do. Listening increases the chance that you will focus on the other person in the present moment, and truly grasp what they feel and need without making assumptions or acting from your own history.

Good listeners defeat the bad habits that prevent them from really listening. Bad habits, such as interrupting, judging, giving advice, taking over, multi-tasking, and reacting to things that push your buttons interfere with your ability to resonate compassion and hope. In addition to overcoming bad listening habits, leaders who listen well, listen in the moment and on behalf of the other person—not from the past and what MIT lecturer William Isaacs calls their "personal net of memories." In his groundbreaking book on dialogue, Isaacs writes "To listen is to realize that much of our reaction to others comes from memory; it is stored reaction, not fresh response at all" (1999, p. 92). When you remove the net of your own memories and listen to people with a fresh mind, you successfully suspend the judgments and resistance that interferes with listening and which make you less compassionate.

Listen to Empower

Leaders who listen also empower others to uncover insights that move them to take action. When acknowledged in this way, listening is actually a powerful leadership development strategy. When I (Elle) teach leadership coaching skills, for example, 100% of the time participants are astonished to learn just how much it means to people when they simply and sincerely listen to them. These leaders are equally surprised and a little bit chagrined to realize just how poor they are at listening. At the end of a listening exercise I led with educational leaders in Zambia, for example, here is what they told me about how it felt to be listened to without interruption, judgment, or resistance:

- It felt like for once, I was able to hear myself think.
- It felt like if I could keep talking, I would figure the whole thing out.
- It felt like my coach really cared about me and what I was facing.
- I realized that what I first thought was the issue really wasn't it at all.
- I heard myself explain the problem I'm facing with greater clarity.
- It felt like someone trusted me to know what to do.
- It felt funny, but knowing I wasn't going to be interrupted, I was able to be more thoughtful about what I said.

Minnesota nurse leader Leslie Parran knows firsthand the power of having a skilled coach who listens well. She says, "When I'm first given a challenge, I have to wrap my mind around it. I have to talk it through with someone who is skilled at engaging me in reflective thought. Then I can talk to my team and engage them better." New York nurse leader Lisa McDonald, who has led important national work on pain protocols for orthopedic surgical patients says, "I think one of the hardest things is to find a person who is going to listen to you, who believes that maybe you are on to something. You have to believe that what you say has meaning and purpose."

Emily Dickinson is quoted as having written to a friend "I felt it shelter to speak with you" (Wineapple, 2009, p. 216). Dickinson's words beautifully express the value of listening. When we listen people feel understood, they feel their ideas matter, they feel less isolated, and in the aftermath of disruptive change, they are more likely to join leaders in creating new pathways toward excellence.

Develop Your Advocacy Voice

Because they can depend on their ability to communicate and persuade others toward action, nurse leaders who have mastered the art of advocacy are also more resonant and therefore, more resilient.

Recalling a time early in her career when caring for a patient with multiple gunshot wounds, who had just returned from surgery, Juli Maxworthy, now an assistant professor at the University of San Francisco, noticed that the woman's chest tube was filling with blood. "It was very clear to me that something was very wrong," says Juli, who called the doctor to tell him his patient was in trouble and needed to go back into surgery. "It was 3:00 A.M. and this particular trauma surgeon was not the nicest person. He came storming in and started chewing on me." Undeterred, and working with a team that respected her skills, Juli had already packed the patient up to send her back into surgery. One hour later, when the patient returned to Juli's unit, the surgeon told her that nothing was wrong. But the trauma nurses told Juli the truth—the patient had a hole in her vena cava that needed repair and Juli's advocacy had saved her life.

The *Code of Ethics for Nurses with Interpretive Statements*, (ANA, 2015) makes it clear that nurses have a responsibility not only to promote, advocate for and strive to protect the health, safety, and rights of patients, but to also advocate on behalf of colleagues and the profession. Reflecting on what builds resilience in nurse leaders, Juli suggests that it begins with the ethical responsibility nurses have toward patient advocacy, which gives them ample opportunities to learn how to mobilize others to action. Juli says,

As nurses, advocacy is part of our job. Being an advocate at every level of your career and in formal leadership roles makes us resilient. We learn to take the flack our physician partners sometime give us, and we learn not to back down.

As the largest professional group within health care, and one recognized by the public as the most trusted profession (Rifkin, 2015), nurse leaders who hone their advocacy skills and skillfully apply them to create necessary change, experience the quality of resonance. Over time, nurses who are skillful advocates gain confidence in their abilities to influence others—becoming even more resonant in the process, and ultimately more resilient. They are more able to build support for change and help others bounce forward.

Nurse leaders who are pros at advocacy have mastered several skills including problem solving, communication, influence, and collaboration and they create a culture that encourages advocacy by others (Tomajan, 2012). In her article titled *Advocating for Nurses and Nursing*, Tomajan writes, "When leaders support open communication, collaboration, and conflict resolution skills, staff are able to advocate more effectively for themselves and for colleagues."

Nurse educator Cathy Coleman says that nurse leaders must also mentor and coach the nurses they lead to claim the informal authority they have through the virtue of their roles, to advocate for what is right and to make a difference. For example, when Cathy was a cancer nurse she remembers feeling troubled when a patient would not receive biopsy results before the weekend, even when Cathy knew they were available. Cathy says, "I knew these patients would worry all weekend so I called the attending physicians so they could call the patient and give them their results. This was an extra step I could take because of my position."

Face Harsh Realities with Optimism

Leaders who resonate optimism spread hope and a spirit of can-do throughout the organization. Nurse leaders who work in high poverty communities, or with very ill or injured patients, and who are inventing solutions to improve wellness for vulnerable populations cannot afford pessimism; they simply must believe they can make a difference. If they did not, it would be much less likely that they would return to work each day and devote themselves to turning things around.

Originating in 1990 with American psychologist Martin Seligman, researchers and scientists from psychology and neurobiology have long studied optimism.

It turns out that most people, unless they suffer from depression (or as in the animals in Seligman's ground-breaking research, learned helplessness), believe they are mostly in control of future events; therefore, they believe they are less at risk of experiencing negative events (such as divorce, getting cancer, or having a car wreck), than other people.

People who pride themselves on their ability to grasp the reality of life and all of its difficulties may choose to view optimism as a soft leadership skill, or one unworthy of serious attention. However, optimism can produce real benefits in the workplace. Research on this phenomenon, known as "The Optimism Bias," shows that it may in fact lead to better outcomes (Sharot, 2012). According to Tombaugh, "Optimistic leaders are more likely to see problems as challenges, exert greater effort for longer periods to reach their goals, and seek out and appreciate the positive aspects of difficult situations" (2005, p. 16).

In the face of harsh realities, leaders who are resilient are optimistic but not naive—they are aware of the difficulties facing them. But instead of focusing cynically on what they cannot do, resilient leaders see what they can do. Rather than complain about what they want less of from others, resilient leaders describe what is needed.

Whereas pessimistic leaders use difficult situations as an excuse to throw up their hands, point fingers, and lose focus, the same appalling information inspires optimistic leaders to action. At no time is this truer than when unpopular change initiatives upset people. Leslie Parran, a nurse leader in Minnesota, shared an anecdote to illustrate this point. Years ago, when Leslie was a director working in a hospital, a decision was made at high levels in the organization to change the care model in several units, including hers. Leslie says,

> *Whether or not I agreed with the decision, I needed to help the affected units find ways to figure out how to make the transition. During times of change like this, you cannot be a leader who adds fuel to the fire. If you do, you encourage inaction, gossip, and rumors.*

Celebrate Small Wins

Resonant leaders move people to action. Therefore, one way to determine your level of leadership resonance is to look at the organization's progress toward and eventual achievement of important goals. Progress toward the goals of the organization can be thought of as small wins. Small wins do not mean small goals; they are incremental gains in the direction you want to go. When small wins occur, they reveal where the organization has traction and where it can leverage early gains into more significant gains.

Small wins are aided by a transparent and consistent approach to measure leadership performance. Consider again the example of nurse leader Sharon Rohrback, where every nurse is given a MacBook that they use to enter data on up to 150 indicators when they visit a mother and baby. Sharon says that data on myriad critical metrics of newborn babies and their vulnerable mothers inspires employees and volunteers to work with passion every day. She says,

> We measure important outcomes which not only give us feedback that our programs are working, but that continue to let us know that the problem is still grave and that we cannot stop our work. It also lets our employees and volunteers know how they make a difference." She adds, "In this high-risk field, it is important to have real-time data. Our nurses do not have to wait for annual results to come in. They just go online and they can see how well we are doing.

Equally important to celebrating small changes in important metrics is for nurse leaders, whose accomplishments are achieved largely through the work of others, to connect growth and progress to the goals that are linked to their evaluation and contract. In order to create resonance, and to inspire others to mobilize around the goals, highly resilient leaders provide updates to their bosses, to boards, and to other stakeholder groups, that explain and demonstrate the connections between seemingly unrelated work and crucial organizational priorities. As one leader put it,

> Every time something is put in motion or accomplished in service of a larger goal, you need to make the connection specific and explicit. The leader literally needs to say, 'this accomplishment is for goal number three' or 'this accomplishment is for goal number six.'

Leaders who draw attention to small wins and who celebrate the people and the strategies that created them, infuse the organization with hope and faith that the vision is achievable. Celebrations of small wins also keep the minds of stakeholders focused on what matters and focused on what they can do to keep progress moving forward rather than what they fear they cannot do.

Recognizing Small Wins

Here are some examples of small wins to look for in nursing. What would you add to this list specific to your organization, department, or initiative?

- Celebrate closing in on a goal—narrowing a gap. Be specific about the percentage changes and include details about the tactics, resources, and people associated with the changes.

- Celebrate the ways individuals and teams make a difference in the field of nursing and for patients through publishing evidence-based research.

- Celebrate the favorite mistakes—those errors and blunders that create an upside of knowledge and insight, those a-ha! moments about how to refine and hone the next approach.

- Celebrate cultural artifacts that represent change. One example might be schedules of multidisciplinary rounding that show a trend toward collaboration. Another might be a data display of increasing satisfaction rates among groups—complete with photos and quotes from patients and families. Another example might be the percentage of nurses that offer peer coaching or mentoring for novice nurses.

- Celebrate behavioral wins. For example, if you want more nurses to view themselves as innovative leaders, post the percentage of point of care research projects underway.

- Celebrate the number or percentage of employees who learned something new and shared it with a wider audience.

- Extend and increase goals and then celebrate the new challenge.

- Peter Senge wrote, "Truly creative people use the gap between vision and current reality to generate energy for change" (1990, p. 153). Therefore, celebrate the number of people who take new action in response to the presentation of a challenging vision. Take surveys once in a while asking "On a scale of 1–5, with 1 being low and 5 being high, how engaged do you feel in our organizational vision?"

- Post data but also include the stories of some of the people behind the numbers. For example, although Nurses for Newborns is sharp at collecting and using data, Sharon Rohrbach says, "To really let people know they are making a difference, you have to include the stories."

- Celebrate craftsmanship—find the nurses who perform challenging procedures and processes exceptionally well and create opportunities for others to observe them before they need to perform the same procedure.

Remember That You Matter to Others

Although neuroscientists have shown that the limbic system is open and that emotions are contagious between people, many leaders fail to act on this knowledge. They go about their workday going from one task to the next without noting just how much they mean to the people around them and the effect they have on them. They miss opportunities to connect with and inspire the people they lead. Nurse leader Lisa McDonald, says that if you don't see yourself as someone who can make a difference, you stop yourself from being innovative. "You think to yourself, 'well, I'm only one person—I don't think I matter.'" Lisa Gifford, a spirited nurse leader and educator who currently lives on a farm in Bosnia and guest lectures in the school of nursing at the University of San Francisco, urges all nurses to take in the relatedness of everything they do and the impact it has on the organization. She says,

> I would tell young nurses to realize that when they are at their best—even when no one is looking—they bring about the best results for patients and for the whole organization.

In order to increase your resonance, it is important for you to be mindful of how much you mean to the people in your personal and professional life. Being mindful that your actions, words, demeanor, and emotions make a difference for others makes you humble and tender. When you are mindful about how much you mean to others, you realize you have power to inspire and transmit courage, and you choose, in every daily interaction, to connect to your own purpose on the planet.

Articulate Well the Vision and Strategies of the Organization

In organizations, vision refers to a clear expression of the future it seeks to create to realize its essential purpose. As a piece of a larger framework that includes the organizational mission and underlying values, shared visions are powerful tools for establishing resonance throughout organizations (Senge, 1990). Leaders who wish to increase their ability to respond to adversity with resilience, therefore, mindfully employ the vision of the organization to create a high level of resonance.

In *Resonant Leadership*, Boyatzis and McKee (2005) emphasize the point that the organizational vision must be shared and it must be inspirational; it must express a better future that drives people to action. Writing in *Fifth Discipline* about how the vision inspires people to action, Peter Senge describes how visions begin to create resonance. He writes "Visions spread because of a reinforcing process of increasing clarity, enthusiasm, communication and commitment. As people talk, the vision grows clearer. As it gets clearer, enthusiasm for its benefits build" (p. 227). Moreover, the leader must understand the vision inside and out. Boyatzis and McKee write "You cannot inspire others about a vision if you yourself cannot articulate it" (p. 164).

When it comes to keeping people focused and pulling in the same direction, resilient leaders doggedly bring every conversation back to the organizational vision. Championing the shared organizational vision is an act of leadership, though as Dean Melnyk points out, a challenging one. Melnyk says,

> *When you are a visionary leader you see things before others see them. People who don't see what you see will poke holes in your ideas—they tell you what can't be done instead of asking how they can help you. So, you have to appeal to them emotionally to get them on board.*

The ability of the organization's vision to reach deep into the passion of so many stakeholders is one reason why it is a powerful tool for creating and sustaining resonance throughout the organization.

Have a Sense of Humor

Often, the hard lessons in life contain the seeds of mirth—even if only in hindsight. Donea Shane, a nurse leader who participated in my (Elle) initial research on the nature of wisdom in nurses (Allison, 2006), loves to use her personal story to inspire and amuse others who are diligently working up the nursing career tract. Before Donea retired, she had worked her way up to one of the highest positions in nursing administration at the University of New Mexico—Dean of the College of Nursing. Her road to the top was anything but smooth, but grace and synchronicity and predictable miracles in the form of people and circumstances provided momentum along the way.

Donea came to nursing through a diploma nursing school instead of through a university program of studies. Donea says, "Coming in from a diploma school background to a baccalaureate faculty was practically like coming into Tiffany's with a Walmart background." At the time, a grant provided the funding stream for her position. Referring to her credentials, Donea's boss (who was dean at the time) told her "You're never going to get on the tenure track and you're never going to be able to stay here when the funding runs out if you don't do something about your credentials." So, her boss coached Donea to start a PhD program in educational administration with her minor in nursing. This proposal proved tougher than it appeared on the surface because the University did not have a master's program in nursing at the time—but the dean was in the process of establishing one so she told Donea to "just get started and see what happens." As grace would have it, the master's program in nursing did come through, which meant that Donea could take those graduate level courses for her PhD minor. The upshot of it all is that Donea eventually became Dean of the College of Nursing without ever really getting a MSN degree—a degree one might reasonably expect a person in her position to have. Laughing, Donea says, "I've got five degrees and not a one of them is quite right. That was the hardest thing about my whole career path...I did not have the right credentials and I was always scrambling."

A sense of humor not only unites people and creates resonance in the environment, but it can lend a healthier perspective to disruptive events from the outset. For example, out of her own beginnings as a nurse from a hospital school, Donea's career (and post-career professional activities) was devoted to supporting the educational process for nurses and especially to "smoothing the way for the RNs coming into the Baccalaureate program."

Having a sense of humor about life's foils helps leaders maintain healthy perspectives about serious situations. This sets a great example for others too— especially when you emphasize the lesson learned and the assumptions you had to drop. Having a self-directed sense of humor lets people see that in spite of your wisdom and experience, you believe that you, like everyone else, can learn something new every day.

Take Care of Yourself

Leaders who become dissonant are usually in desperate need of renewal. They have neglected their own health and emotional needs in favor of their work and it shows: They are pessimistic, tired, cranky, impatient, and fragile. These leaders make more mistakes and poorer decisions. They alienate people and undermine relationships, which in turn undermines their leadership resilience.

Even when work is meaningful, leaders who respond to constant streams of stress by working harder and giving more, ultimately experience distress and may even burn themselves out. Boyatzis and McKee call this pattern of stress without renewal "the syndrome of sacrifice, stress and dissonance" (p. 7). When leaders become dissonant, they contribute to unhealthy stress within the organization, which only compounds their troubles and continues and deepens the syndrome. The way out of dissonance is through renewal (the subject of the previous chapter).

Summary

Whether you are a veteran leader or a novice leader, striving toward resonance will make you more resilient. Leaders become more resilient by asking thoughtful leadership questions and through listening to people talk about their experience while remaining aware of and regulating their own emotions. At the same time, these leaders focus on broadcasting a compelling vision of the future, often referring to the emotional investment of themselves and others in the vision. Resonant leaders develop an awareness of how they inspire—or don't inspire—others, and they take steps to cultivate emotional styles that move people to action.

Activities and Questions

1. Recall an occasion when you were keenly aware that your emotional state of being was being corrupted by someone else's dissonance. What do you remember feeling and thinking? What happened next—were you able to pull yourself out of spiraling into dissonance, or did you lose your balance and equanimity? Either way, what were your interactions with others like immediately afterward? How did you feel after those interactions?

2. Pay attention to the first inkling of destructive emotions such as anger, fear, and attachment (the inability to accept the temporary nature of everything) and stare back at these destructive emotions (recognize them for what they are) and redirect your thoughts.

3. When you are in a difficult or unpleasant situation, do you maintain your presence, or do you either disengage and shut down or become overly aggressive for the situation?

4. What do you add to meetings or gatherings? How would others answer this question about you?

5. What makes you dissonant? What impact does it have on others when you are fearful, angry, or without hope or faith?

6. What does it take for you to pull yourself out of a dissonant funk? Once you decide to become more resonant, how long does it take you to do so?

7. How do you know when you are headed toward a dissonant state of mind? What patterns are present in the hours preceding this?

8. Who do you know who is really great to be with? Why exactly is that? What does this person do? What does he or she say? What does his or her presence do for you? Do you think differently or feel differently around this person?

9. What emotions describe your family, organization, or work team? How many would you say are positive, such as happy, optimistic, excited, creative, kind, and generous? How many would you say are negative, such as fearful, depressed, lonely, secretive, jealous, or miserly?

10. Who in your own life would benefit from a compassionate perspective? Who empathizes with you but also has constructive input for you to think about? Who needs your compassionate perspective?

11. Pick an important innovation or strategy in your organization and list all of goals it is designed to improve. List the incremental wins that have brought you closer to the goal. Remember, small wins are more of what you want to see—even in big goals that you are far from completing.

12. Brainstorm ways to commemorate small and early wins that involve the people doing the work and the people whose lives are made better as a result of the work. Let them tell the stories about how things are going and the positive changes that have occurred.

13. Stop talking about your circle of control (which is likely an illusion) and start talking about your circle of influence.

5

Relationships

Surround Yourself with Good Souls

The moment we cease to hold each other, the
sea engulfs us and the light goes out.

—American writer James Baldwin (1924–1987)

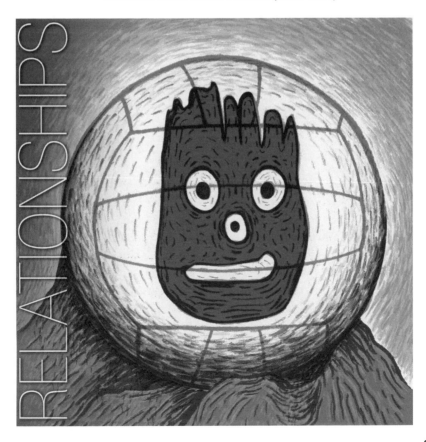

We open this chapter with a story from Dan, who, as a product of the Army Student Nurse Program, discovered firsthand the importance of relationships to leadership resilience:

Once I graduated from my baccalaureate program in 1975, I was assigned to the US Army Institute for Surgical Research at Brooke Army Medical Center in San Antonio, Texas. Working with burn patients was most challenging. I realized early on that the stress of the treatment procedures—painful debridements and numerous surgeries and skin grafts took its toll on patients, families, and staff members.

Six months into my tour of duty I realized I was not prepared with the knowledge I needed to help the patients and families cope with the psychological traumas of burn injuries. I returned to school to learn more about psychiatric-mental health nursing. I also became very interested in alternative and complementary treatment modalities, the impact and influence of stress on recovery and how the doctors, nurses and corpsmen managed to cope with the day to day stressors of dealing with painful procedures, scarring disfigurement and often death. There is camaraderie among doctors and nurses who work in trauma and critical care and it is very evident that relationships are key to navigating the stress and strain of working in a critical care area. Relationships are key.

Researchers who study post-traumatic growth would not be surprised by the esprit de corps among healthcare personnel who work as teams in high-intensity care environments. Their studies show that people who come through adversity and ultimately feel stronger experience a heightened awareness of just how much the people in their lives and the networks they belong to mean to them. Anyone who has been a part of a high-functioning healthcare team knows from instinct and experience that linked networks of relationships make them more resilient. The lesson for novice and veteran nurse leaders alike is profound: You must resist buying into the cliché that it is lonely at the top. Even if your nature leans toward introversion, you must mindfully form and nurture relationships that sustain you and support you when adversity strikes. Don't settle for anything less.

The Relationship Inventory

Before reading on, take a few moments to respond to the relationship inventory (to take the online version, visit www.WisdomOut.com) depicted in Exercise 5.1, which will provide you with objective feedback about your current state of relationship.

Instructions. Respond to each of the following statements quickly, providing your first impulse as the answer. If you are responding as a team, look at the average response or look at the amount of responses for each number in the range. A response of 10 is the strongest possible agreement, and 1 is the strongest possible disagreement. There are no correct answers.

Reflection on Your Score
Take a moment to reflect on the results of your Relationship Inventory.

My Relationship Inventory Score is: _____

Highlight key insights from the score interpretation you received. What sounds right to you? What seems off? What goals do you want to set for yourself or for your team?

Interpreting Your Score
Where do highly resilient people tend to score on the Relationship Inventory? Leaders who take the online version of the Relationship Inventory, and who also rate themselves high on happiness and meaningful work, score most often in the range of 71–100.

If You Score in the Range of 10–40: You claim to embrace a rugged individualism, but the reality is that yours is a sad, lonely, and difficult life. You perceive the people around you as being dense, difficult, and corrupt; they disappoint you at every turn. Sometimes you'd like to confide in someone, but if you took that risk your partner might leave you, your friends would make fun of you, and your colleagues at work would use it against you. So you never risk being authentic. As a result of your isolation, your emotional and physical health may be suffering.

If You Score in the Range of 41–70: You consider yourself nobody's fool. Several times you have given friends and colleagues the benefit of the doubt, and you've been burned. Up to a point, you are supportive, accepting, and nonjudgmental, but after a while it feels as if you're the only one doing the work in these relationships, and it's just not fair that you bear the burden of sustaining them. When it comes to new relationships at work and in your personal life, you're really on the fence. You often take a wait and see approach before you decide who to accept, appreciate, and trust. In summary, when it comes to relationships you are cautious. On occasion, relationships are a

Exercise 5.1. The Relationship Inventory

Statement	Strongly Disagree									Strongly Agree
1. I have at least one close personal relationship where it is safe to be who I am, without any acting or pretending.	1	2	3	4	5	6	7	8	9	(10)
2. In my professional life, I have at least one relationship in which I can accept negative feedback without any threat to the relationship.	1	2	3	4	5	6	7	8	9	(10)
3. I can be very hurt by or disappointed with someone close to me, forgive him or her, and still maintain a close relationship.	1	2	3	4	5	6	(7)	8	9	10
4. When I hear other people speak with contempt about someone close to them, it makes me very uncomfortable.	1	2	3	4	5	6	7	8	(9)	10
5. When I feel like a failure, I know someone I can talk to who will not judge me as a failure.	1	2	3	4	5	6	7	8	9	(10)
6. I can recall a conversation within the past couple of weeks in which I simply listened to the other person without interruption.	1	2	3	4	5	6	7	8	(9)	10
7. My closest colleagues at work know that they can occasionally blow off steam with me and that I will forgive them, even if they are a little bit out of control.	1	2	3	4	5	6	7	8	9	(10)
8. Some of my closest relationships are with people who give me candid advice, even when their candor hurts a little bit.	1	2	3	4	5	6	7	8	(9)	10
9. I can almost always think of something encouraging and nice to say to other people.	1	2	3	4	5	6	7	8	(9)	10
10. I have personally expressed gratitude to a person close to me at least once in the past week.	1	2	3	4	(5)	6	7	8	9	10

Total Score: 88

struggle for you. This usually has to do with the perception you hold that others have let you down. You can improve in relationships by being more clear and specific about what you are trying to accomplish and what you need from others to be successful. Remember, people cannot read your mind, so you must be willing to ask for help and show gratitude for help received.

If You Score in the Range of 71–100: You may not have thousands of friends, but you are very fortunate to have people in your personal and professional life who are true friends. You can confide in them and they in you. You attract these people because you too are a true friend, giving time, acceptance, and gratitude to others. If you scored in the 90s, then you are living by the Platinum Rule, giving more to others than you expect them to give to you. When you need their support, these supportive relationships will be there for you. The liability for you is that other less resilient people (who do not accomplish goals in their own work and life) may take advantage of you. This means that to be even more resilient as a leader, you need to give yourself permission to extend your energy to those relationships that are reciprocal and trustworthy and cut ties with those that diminish your ability to accomplish great things.

How Relationships Make Us Resilient

In the film *Castaway*, Tom Hanks stars as Chuck Noland, the lone survivor of a Federal Express plane crash. Early in the film, a large box from the plane's cargo washes up on the island where Noland has found refuge. Noland opens the box with a knife, slicing his hand in the process. Still bleeding, Noland lifts out a volleyball made by the Wilson athletic company, leaving a bloody handprint that reminds him of a head with crazy-looking hair. In a moment of playfulness, given the severity of his situation, he draws in eyes, nose, and a mouth, and names the ball "Wilson." As unusual as a relationship between a person and volleyball might be, Wilson is Noland's constant companion. When Noland figures out how to make a fire, Wilson is there. When Noland catches his first fish and enjoys his first real meal since washing up on the island, Wilson watches by the fire. And when Noland builds the raft that eventually takes him back out to sea in search of rescue, Wilson is there too. With Wilson by his side, Chuck Noland is able to take necessary action in order to survive. Wilson gave Noland courage.

Relationships Give Us Courage

As presented in Chapter 1, the hardships that confront nurse leaders are neither rare nor unusual. Any day, anything can happen and as the wonderful

Beatles song goes, we get by with a little help from our friends. Dependable networks of relationships are sources of courage; they give leaders confidence to move forward when they would rather stay in bed.

Nurse leader Marcia McCormick, program director of three adult inpatient mental health units in Minnesota, speaks fondly of Pat Murphy, another director in the program. Previously, Pat was actually Marcia's supervisor. But when their hospital merged some programs and responsibilities, going from four managers to two, Marcia and Pat found themselves working close together, both as directors. Marcia says:

> From the very beginning, we decided that neither of us could do our jobs alone. So we had lunch together every day and we became very good friends. We also decided very deliberately, that we would not compete with each other. For example, if one of us wants to offer a workshop, we pull together and offer it to both of our staffs. If one of us isn't available to answer questions or provide support to our teams, the other one will.

Marcia and Pat are exceptional role models for how relationships enable resilience. Together, they make the units they lead stronger, less fragile, and less stressful for them and for their units.

Relationships Promote Emotional and Physiological Well-Being

It turns out the relationships that form your networks and give you courage also sustain your heart and mind. They promote good physical and mental health, which keeps you living longer and with sharper cognitive faculties (Jetten, Haslam, Alexander, & Branscombe, 2009; Ozbay et al., 2007).

For most people, close relationships are a source of happiness and comfort. They provide safe harbor from life's troubles. In their book *Loneliness: Human Nature and the Need for Social Connection* (2008), John Cacioppo and William Patrick write about the impact of prolonged loneliness on individuals and society. They suggest that connections with other people contribute to a person's ability to think, exert will power, persevere during tough times, and regulate emotions. And in the book titled *Bowling Alone: The Collapse and Revival of American Community* (2000), Robert Putnam writes, "As a rough rule of thumb, if you belong to no groups but decide to belong to one, you cut your risk of dying over the next year in half" (p. 331).

Relationships, however, do more than strengthen us emotionally. New findings indicate they also improve our physiological well-being. For example, social neuroscience experts Cacioppo and Patrick found that loneliness could have as detrimental an impact on a person's health as obesity or smoking. On the other hand, loving relationships that ward off loneliness can positively reduce several health problems, including cardiovascular disease (Lynch, 2000). Other researchers found that having friends appears to increase immune system responses to flu shots in college students, while the lack of social connections reduces the benefits of exercise. (Zolli & Healy 2012). Zolli and Healy sum up the impact of relationships on personal well-being when they write "Social isolation is not just bad for our psychological well-being. It appears to leave its trace at the cellular level" (p. 130).

Who Are Your Wilsons?

The odd but lifesaving friendship we see between Wilson and Noland in the film *Castaway* provides a poignant example of the importance of relationships. And as Dan reflects back on his early career, the healthcare team at the Brooke Army Medical Center, Institute for Surgical Research, enabled the team to cope with trauma and turn difficult and challenging experiences into learning opportunities.

When Dan decided that he needed to go back to school to learn more about the effects of trauma, he struck a deal with his chief nurse, Jean Truscott. Jean supported his plan to work a permanent evening and night shift schedule so he could go to school during the day. In 18 months Dan finished his master's degree in psychiatric nursing and was able to create a new role in the burn unit as a psychiatric clinical nurse specialist. Several people were instrumental in this innovation including the chief nurse, Jean Truscott, and Commander of the Burn Unit operations, Dr. Basil Pruitt. Additionally, the unit's chaplain, psychologist, and all the enlisted people on the unit supported Dan, as did nurse colleagues and healthcare workers.

Every day, nurse leaders at all levels must respond to challenges with resilience. And they can't do it alone. These leaders need to ask themselves, "Who are my Wilsons?" Equally important, nurse leaders must ask, "Whose 'Wilson List' am I on?" Nurse leader and educator Sara Guido from the University of San Francisco is a "Wilson" to the nurses she teaches. Sara says,

> *I have the opportunity to work in the clinical setting with students and their patients. This is where I do a lot of mentoring especially for nurses who have hopes and dreams and aspirations but who may work in a setting where they do not have equal opportunities to grow. Through mentoring, I can bridge this gap for someone's son or daughter who is just starting in nursing.*

A relationship has to do with the process leaders use to bond with and bridge people inside and outside the organization, who form valuable networks that generate social capital (Knoke, 1999; Nahapiet & Ghoshal, 1998). Social capital can include resources, introductions to the right people, friendship, and love. When leaders leverage their networks in service of strategic goals that accomplish meaningful work, they influence the entire organization (Ibarra & Hunter, 2007).

Relationships That Provide Love

Some relationships provide love. *Late Bloomers* is a Swiss film about 80-year-old Marta, a former seamstress who decides, in spite of interference from her stuffy son and neighbors, to turn her late husband's grocery store into a racy and elegant lingerie shop. Lucky for Marta, she has four friends, including Lisi, who stand by her and will not let her give up. At one turning point in the film, Marta's son ransacks and closes her shop. That's when beautiful and flamboyant Lisi, who is frequently scorned and ridiculed by people in the village herself, encourages Marta to carry on. Marta gratefully tells her friend "Lisi, you are such a good soul."

Veteran educational leader Carmen Franco told me (Elle)

> It is important for leaders to follow negative experiences with positive experiences. If they don't, they risk inaction; they may not get up again. You need someone in your life who has your back. Leaders who are truly alone may not make it.

Like Marta, resilient leaders have good souls in their lives who unconditionally believe in them. These networks of family members, friends, and coworkers believe that you can accomplish anything you put your mind to. They are always there to listen and reflect your dearest dreams back to you. Because these networks of people who love you expect you to succeed, they ask questions that point you toward your goals and might even scold you if you waver in your self-confidence.

From 1984–1987, as the Director of Nursing of the William S. Hall Psychiatric Institute in Columbia, South Carolina, Dan worked side by side with a 37-year veteran of the mental health department—a diploma-prepared psychiatric-mental health nurse named Florence Cromer. Florence was a very wise woman and experienced nurse with a great way of tempering some of Dan's enthusiasms and plans. When she sensed that he was moving too fast or too quickly with changes she would pause and say, "Dr. Pesut, Dr. Pesut, I learned a long time ago that there is the ideal, and the real, and then what you can live with." Basically, this was Florence's way of shaping and influencing as well as supporting and cautioning Dan to think twice about moving too rapidly with a change or innovation for which there may or may not have been support. When Florence retired, Dan was invited to deliver some remarks and he highlighted and memorialized Florence's sage advice creating something he called Cromer's Law: $R = (I \cdot R) \div$ Values. Reality is a function of the Ideal times the Real divided by one's Values (beliefs) and what one can live with. Dan still values, appreciates, and remembers Cromer's law and is forever grateful that Florence had his back as she both supported and challenged his leadership initiatives.

Relationships That Support You with Resources
Leaders gain strength for themselves and for their communities of practice when they petition their network of relationships for support.

Resilient leaders recognize a bountiful universe, but they also do the good and difficult work needed to draw support for their cause. Leaders who nurture their networks when things are going well can draw on them in times of need. Sometimes, what leaders need in order to carry on comes in the form of skills, information, or mentoring. For example, one nurse leader named Carol, who was not an experienced grant writer, had the opportunity to write a proposal to receive funds to begin a wellness program. Nervous that she would not be successful, Carol gratefully met with Bill, an acquaintance from one of her business networks, who regularly wrote grants to run his nonprofit organization. Bill reviewed Carol's proposal before she submitted it and suggested crucial revisions that won Carol's department the grant funds they sought.

Carol was smart to connect with someone from her network who possessed superb grant proposal writing skills and was willing to be of support to her. But sometimes leaders don't know the right people to turn to. In these cases, it is important to know people who know the right people.

Relationships That Open Doors
Much of what happens in the world happens through the amazing connections people have with each other (Sanders, 2002). These connections form social capital between leaders, constituencies, and enterprises from diverse segments of the community and they knit together networks of support in service of the purpose of the organization.

Cohen & Prusak (2004) define social capital as "the stock of active connections among people; the trust, mutual understanding, and shared values and behaviors that bind members of human networks and communities and make cooperative action possible" (p. 4). Robert Putnam (2000) describes two types of social capital: bonding and bridging. Bonding social capital supports identity formation. Bonding social capital breeds solidarity, supports inclusion, and fosters intra-professional and group loyalty. In contrast, bridging social capital moves beyond bonding of group identity and focuses on linkage of networks of people across various levels of identity, purpose, and missions. Both bonding and bridging social capital support network development, knowledge exchange, and a sense of community. The greater one's social capital the richer one's network, resources, and sense of community.

Leaders who are serious about success, but squeamish about networking, must learn to make connections that matter (Baber & Waymon, 2007). When they do, these leaders realize that networks of support are created not through unseemly schmoozing, but through sincere interactions that create social capital. Nurse leader and educator Rachelle Larsen cultivates authentic networks of relationships by participating on cross-departmental committees both within her college and within the community, thus putting herself "in the know" when new needs arise. She says, "When I am looking to place nursing students in the community, these committees are often the source of ideas about new clinical rotations for students, who also get to be part of a solution to something that is needed."

Beware of Relationships With Non-Resilient Individuals

As open as resilient leaders are to other people, they are not indiscriminate when deciding on whom they will spend their energy. Resilient leaders do not choose to spend an enormous amount of energy on single individuals who are strengthened by attention for behavior that weakens others. In work and in life, individuals who indulge in self-serving behaviors that seek to undermine good work and positive change can also undermine leadership resilience. These individuals might create a lot of noise in the system, but they are usually non-productive in their own work and lives; thus, they are non-resilient.

For example, Juan, who is the head of the professional learning center in a multi-hospital corporation, put an enormous amount of his staff's time and energy into developing a cutting-edge leadership academy to grow new leaders in the member hospitals. Amidst a fair amount of pomp and bluster, the CNO of the largest hospital, Kris, insisted on certain allowances and adaptations to the program. She also insisted on priority enrollment to the

Characteristics of Non-Resilience
(In Others or in Yourself)

- Not achieving goals

- Not following through on agreements

- Making commitments in order to impress others in the moment, but not with an intention to follow through

- A lack of grit when it comes to following through or following up on nitty-gritty details

- Sloppy work when it comes down to unglamorous but required tasks

- Blustery beginnings that fizzle

- A wake of strained and fractured relationships with others

- Other people do not want to collaborate with them

- Being a gossip-monger

- Taking credit for the work of others

program, claiming the first two academies for her hospital alone. Juan and his team did their best to accommodate Kris, even though it delayed implementation of the program and put some of the other hospitals at a disadvantage. Finally, when the leadership academy was to launch, without providing explanation, Kris cancelled both of the academies she had agreed to. In addition, she seemed oblivious to the fact that the professional learning center now had to scramble to fill the vacant slots that she initially claimed. Moreover, Kris did not seem to know or care when the leaders in her organization caught wind of the incident and lamented the loss of a quality leadership academy. She just blustered on to the next big idea.

Although Kris fancied herself as a dynamic and assertive leader who went after resources and support for her district, she neglected to see that she followed through on very few commitments and therefore accomplished very little. She also neglected to notice the battered relationships she left behind. Meanwhile, Juan and his staff learned a valuable lesson: Energy spent on non-resilient individuals is energy unwisely spent.

While we should have compassion for those who are non-resilient, we also must recognize them and employ strategies to minimize their power to undermine progress and good work. If you cannot eliminate the need to work with or rely on these people at all, ways to mitigate the impact of non-resilient individuals include securing clear and written agreements, identifying shorter milestones, employing the use of dependent flowcharts (where one thing must be accomplished before the next thing can occur), limiting their involvement in and responsibility for critical outcomes, setting up contingencies, and building in redundancies and simultaneous efforts that mitigate the fallout when the non-resilient individual lets you down. (See the sidebar on next page for a summary of non-resilience characteristics.)

Resilient leaders do not accomplish great things by wasting energy on people and programs that hinder and halt positive change for a greater good. Resilient leaders know where they can make the greatest difference, and they create strong networks of other resilient individuals who are also known for getting things done.

Cultivating the Leadership Resilience-Enabler Relationships

In many cases, the lack of reliable networks is the root cause of a leader's inability to mobilize support for initiatives when facing resistance. Even leaders with undeniably clear and compelling visions that have the greater good at heart can find themselves stunned to learn they do not have support from key individuals in their lives and in the system.

Not surprisingly, resilient leaders have a knack for cultivating important relationships in service of their organizations (Fullan, 2008). Leaders who develop skills in connecting with people and groups have learned how to create the right chemistry that gains them access to support and resources they lack through their own connections. Here are a few ways to develop your skills in creating the chemistry needed to form networks:

> **Be mindful about what you say.** Have the courage to speak respectfully even about hot topics, but watch what you say and how you say it. Ask yourself if the words you are about to speak move people closer together or further apart.
>
> **Be open.** Inquire into differing perspectives and know when to agree to disagree.
>
> **Persist in helping people understand the facts.** Be fluent and accurate in expressing your successes and challenges. Point out existing resources and enumerate gaps in resources. Provide information at every opportunity. Engage candidly about what you need from others, and what you do not want or need.

Reflect the best of what other people and groups do back to them.
Point out and celebrate what people and other groups do well. This will help
them build their resilience capacity, which makes everyone stronger.

Facilitate connections. Listen and learn the needs of other groups in the
network and connect them with each other. Hone your ability to see connections systemically and broker relationships between groups.

Treat people as if they matter. Stop and interact with people, even those
who appear to lack resources for your cause. Not only might they be
delightful people to know, but they may have other connections that can
be of aid to you down the road. Assume people want to help. Reciprocate
sincerely when people need your support and when you are able to give it.

**Articulate the current state of your department or organization
compared to the ideal vision, and do so regularly, repeatedly, and
consistently.** Two things mobilize people to action: absolute dissatisfaction
with the current situation, and having a vision of something far better. When
you describe both the current state and the vision of your organization to
others, they see both the opportunities and the challenges and more ways to
be of support.

Take care of your reputation. The best way to do this is to follow through
on your commitments and do everything you undertake as well as you can.

**Share your aspirational, big ideas—even those that seem crazy or
impossible.** Progress occurs when good ideas receive the energy they need
to move to the next level. Resilient leaders ensure progress through skillful
advocacy of big ideas that capture the passion of their networks, both inside
and outside the organization.

Help people learn. Leaders who mentor and coach others, empower them,
and make them stronger and able to contribute to common goals.

Coach someone who needs to think through an important challenge.
Resilient leaders are coaching leaders who build the capacity for leadership in others. Leaders who coach know that listening builds relationships.
Therefore, resist giving advice and resist giving your answer to the problem.
Instead, just listen.

**Follow up with the people you supervise and with those whom you
delegate important responsibilities to.** Nurse leaders who coach their
direct reports create powerful relationships where any topic can come up
and any challenge can be faced.

Resilience as a Social Identity

When nurse leaders connect with others in the face of loss, they also establish
a precedent for how to connect with each other when facing challenges in the
future. During times of challenge, your leadership resilience can strengthen
the networks you belong to.

Nurse leader Nan Ybarra reflects back on her experience of being a new nurse leader during Hurricane Ike. Nan says, "It's true that what doesn't kill you can make you stronger." At the time, Nan was a nurse leader in one of the hospitals near the Texas coast that decided not to evacuate patients. The previous manager had been in the role for twenty years and Nan, as the new kid on the block, was still held at arm's length by the nurses in the unit. When Ike hit, Nan threw herself into operating the unit and making decisions to keep patients and nurses safe. Nan says:

> This really was a turning point for me as far as how people related to me and to each other. Before Ike, I felt some resistance to me and to my ideas. With Ike, the staff saw that I was going to keep going. It changed the culture—we all knew we could handle anything together.

Efficacy certainly is a by-product of handling challenges well. When individuals and groups gain awareness about how they are effective, they are galvanized to handle whatever comes their way. More importantly, however, their identity transforms: They step more fully into being people and teams known for the way they handle challenges.

Be a Good Soul

Just as you have good souls in your life who love you, provide you with resources, and open doors for you during times of adversity, you increase resilience for all when you are a good soul to others. Lisa Price, a nurse leader from Oakland, California tells of a colleague who became seriously ill, a senior nurse leader who asked that the staff who reported to her provide her nursing care. Lisa had to carefully make decisions about who would be on the team and who would be the care manager. Lisa says,

> This was a difficult time—how to manage an internal death of this magnitude? But it brought us together as a staff and I gained a lot of respect in a different way from before, for my team. How we care for each other during these situations makes us stronger.

Summary

Relationships are good for you emotionally and physiologically. They give you courage, and they make you stronger especially during times of disruptive change. When adversity strikes, your networks of relationships will want to be of support, but only if you make them a priority when life is smooth and calm. Resilient leaders look to the vision, mission, and prioritized strategies of their organizations, and they identify the relationships likely to come into play. Then, resilient leaders will prioritize these relationships and take steps to sincerely grow them in advance of the agenda.

Activities and Questions

1. People come into our lives to teach us, to challenge us, to support us, and to help us grow. Either working alone or as a team, make a list of the people and organizations that are new to you in your work and life. These individuals may be new faculty and staff, new bosses, new board members, new students, or new community groups. They could be new partnerships, new liaisons, or new advisers. Reflect on what these individuals bring to your organization at this time and what they need from you. Reflect on what you and your organization could learn from them.

2. Think about the 10 most important people in your life. How often do you initiate interactions with them where you ask them what they are working on and what their latest successes have been? Out of these 10, who will you check in with in the next month?

3. What do you have to give to others? Do you have expertise and knowledge that a colleague needs? Who needs your talents and skills in order to accomplish their important work and serve the goals of the organization?

4. Who needs you to listen to them as they process something important or troublesome in their life or work? What do you wish someone would listen to you about?

5. What do you need to learn or have from someone else that would allow you to lead through a specific challenge? Who do you know whom you can ask for help with this?

6. Who do you need to thank for what they have given you or taught to you or shown to you through their example? Thank five people every day and when you do, tell them specifically what you are grateful for. Example: "When you showed me how you set up the timeline for that project, I had a breakthrough on the project I am working on. Thank you for sharing your expertise with me."

7. Have you lost important relationships in your life either with a colleague or family member? How did it happen? On the other hand, have you repaired an important relationship in your life? What actions did you take to do this?

8. What do you love about the work you do? What specifically do you love about the tasks, the processes, and the relationships involved in your work?

9. Who inspires you? Who do you inspire? Who would love for you to notice them, and what would that allow them to do or how would they think differently about themselves?

10. How good are you at meeting your obligations and commitment to others? Do you follow through on promises? Do others consider you or your team trustworthy? Can you be counted on?

11. Who loves you, and who do you love? What does this tell you about yourself? Try to describe in words what you mean to others.

III

Leadership Resilience in Action

6

Stay Calm

Doing nothing is better than being busy doing nothing.

—Lao Tzu

Reminder: As you read this chapter, note where the ideas and strategies presented draw on the leadership resilience-enabling capacities of relationships, resonance, and renewal. Then, at the end of the chapter, write down what you want to learn about or experience in order to bolster the capacities so that you are better able to respond in the aftermath of adversity and disruptive change.

When nurse leader Vanessa got wind that top management was about to require greater accountability about how waste material made it into hazardous bags in the surgical centers, she just about had a fit. She knew the nursing and medical teams would expect her to intervene and stop the idea from becoming practice. What the staff didn't know, though, was that upper management was pressuring Vanessa to support every cost-saving idea they had. The truth is, Vanessa knew that sorting hazardous waste properly would likely save thousands of dollars each fiscal quarter. But getting the already stressed out surgical staff to comply would be quite a struggle. As Vanessa was pondering her next move, the surgical center nurse manager, Antoine, stopped by to inquire about another matter. Knowing that Antoine would not support the new initiative if it indeed came to pass, Vanessa told him what the top management was up to. Predictably, the news distressed and agitated Antoine. He told Vanessa "I'm going to bring this up to the rest of team so we can nip this in the bud NOW." *Oops,* thought Vanessa, *I should have kept my big mouth shut. This is now a train wreck about to happen.*

Vanessa is learning the hard way that when disruptive change occurs, it is often best to first do nothing. As it turns out, this is hard enough. This first phase of the resilience cycle, Stay Calm, demands that you use your higher mind to steady yourself in the immediate aftermath of adversity. As such, it is perhaps the most personal phase in the non-directional cycle of Leadership Resilience in Action. Despite its personal nature, your ability to stay calm is quite visible to those you lead, and it sets an emotional tone that empowers you and others. As nurse leader Lisa McDonald says, "When people react it causes a commotion. Reactions cause people to scatter and it creates new problems."

As with all the actions in the cycle, you will return to Stay Calm again and again as you respond to disruptive change.

First Do Nothing

Some people might think that doing nothing is inappropriately passive or shows weakness. This is because in order to assure our survival, our brains have evolved a strong bias toward negativity—a powerful urge to vigilantly monitor and react to changes around us, and a tendency to recall negative experiences more often than positive experiences (Ariely, 2010, Hansen, 2013). Therefore, when we do not react immediately to disruptive change, it makes us edgy; we think we are putting ourselves in danger and that we are not doing our job. Worse, we worry that doing nothing in place of reacting causes others to suspect we are not up to the demands of leadership.

According to behavioral economist Dan Ariely, who wrote an article titled "The Long Term Effects of Short Term Emotions" for the 2010 online *Harvard Business Review*, the automatic reactions and impulses we initially feel in the face of adversity could cause exactly the wrong response. Ariely says when we find ourselves in a fix, we rifle our minds for "a precedent among past actions without regard to whether a decision was made in emotional or unemotional circumstances" (paragraph 3). This means that if we behaved a certain way in the past, we are likely to behave the same way in the future, even when our reaction and the current situation are mismatched. We are wired to react and act out habits and emotional patterns that may or may not be useful, but that fit like a comfortable pair of shoes. Resisting the urge to react from the past is what makes doing nothing so challenging for most of us.

Rest assured, doing nothing is not taking the easy way out. As one nurse leader, who wishes to go by the name Love and Light, says, "We have to empty our minds which means we also have to learn to care for ourselves. If we don't, we live our lives from a place of fear and then we can't be good leaders." Love and Light adds, "When negative thoughts come to mind, I replace [them] with a positive thought. This helps me recognize that everything we tell ourselves is just a story and we can change the story."

Doing nothing is emotionally and cognitively demanding and is a hallmark of leadership resilience. While less resilient leaders become frenetic or withdraw in the face of disruptive change, resilient leaders first allow themselves time to absorb the information. One leader said,

> Unless we're talking about a crisis, I wait and watch and listen. Sometimes what seems to be a problem at first glance really isn't at all—or if there is a problem the new information helps me make better decisions.

Referencing the 1999 film *The Matrix*, nurse leader Connie Hill offers a vivid and playful strategy for "doing nothing." Connie says, "I picture it like going into slow motion, like in *The Matrix*. When I go into slow motion, I can absorb all the information around me and understand what is really going on. Then I respond with leadership."

Neurologically, during this pause, resilient leaders reroute their emotional responses back to the thinking part of the brain where a dose of rationality is injected into the mix. This neural pause empowers leaders to actively resist the automatic reactions that arise in their agitated minds.

Regulate Your Emotions to Serve Others

After a round of budget-trimming initiatives, nurse leader Carrie had to break some tough news to her department at the college of nursing: the new dean made the decision to eliminate the budget for a special program to create a resource center for rural and economically disadvantaged women living with autoimmune diseases. The project had begun two years earlier when two of her DNP students proposed that they research the impact of lupus on the daily lives of women and launch a project to develop and coordinate state resources for them. Carrie, who had been diagnosed with rheumatoid arthritis herself a few years back, jumped at the chance to support and champion the idea.

Although Carrie knew all along that the program needed grants to run, she had worked hard to elevate the project to a strategy under the university hospital outcome of increasing multi-cultural community outreach and communication, while securing a budget to supplement the grants. Without a budget, she would be unable to pay the nurses who were coordinating a state summit where women could come to participate in focus groups, hear speakers, interact with other women and share ideas and resources.

Carrie began to strategize how to present the news to the DNP students leading the program and to the rest of the faculty. Knowing that people follow her emotional lead, Carrie thought about how she could simultaneously acknowledge the loss while projecting an appropriate amount of what she calls "can-doism." When she met with the nursing students the next day, Carrie told them that a challenge came up for the project that they needed to focus on. In the end, the students put together a virtual conference where women from all over the state participated from their own computers or from libraries and community centers that agreed to participate in the project. Surprisingly, the virtual event drew even more women than they would have had at a live event. Over several months, the grad students continually invited the women to respond to various prompts about living with autoimmune diseases. They followed up with women who had unique ideas and resources—some of the women even started their own blogs. Carrie reflects on what she did to create positive outcomes in spite of losing the budget:

> It really goes back to how you react in the first place. If you act like the situation is hopeless as the leader, other people will act as if it is hopeless too. If you go into problem-solving mode, then others look at it as something that can be solved too.

Regulating one's emotions is not the same thing as being morosely stoic, eerily calm, void of feeling, or sentimentally flat. To do so would devalue the real emotions people feel in the face of disruptive change and would undermine relationships and action in the new reality. The Latin root of the word emotion is *emovere*—something that sets the mind in motion. Leaders who are weak in regulating their emotions are often seized by feelings that overpower them and then limit their range of response. And, as we know from experts in neurobiology and psychology, emotions are contagious (Goleman, 2011). In groups, the person displaying the strongest emotions sets the tone for others, but on teams and in organizations, the most powerful person in the group, such as the designated leader, sets the emotional tone. Leaders who are overcome by emotions such as fear, anger, impatience, and pride, for example, experience a diminished or skewed sense of empowerment and efficacy which they transmit to others (Caruso & Salovey, 2004).

Leading by Setting the Emotional Tone

Leaders carry a great responsibility: Not only do they set the emotional tone for the organization in times of turbulence, but they must discern and show the appropriate emotion—the one that helps people move forward, that helps them heal, that allows them to embrace the reality of the situation, that draws them into new realities. For example, nurse leader Connie Hill says,

> My first reaction with unexpected events occur is to take it all in. Then after I have the complete story, I call someone I know such as my sister who is a CEO and can be a sounding board. I also go to the people who are great sounding boards for me but who are also the key stakeholders in the change. I run things past them and listen to what they think. The added advantage of this approach is I begin to learn what my first followers—those people who will show others how to move forward—are thinking and feeling.

Leaders like Connie who put strategies in place to keep their cool during times of unexpected adversity monitor their emotions in order to positively affect others. They thoughtfully identify what it will take to bring people closer together. They identify the results they want to achieve and then identify what people need from them to act with confidence.

Consider the statements below that present emotions demonstrated by the leader, and the possible positive responses they could catalyze in others:

- Leaders who show a sense of humor when recognizing or acknowledging a mistake catalyze creativity instead of fear in others.
- Leaders who express sadness activate healing for others.
- Leaders who display enthusiasm mobilize a sense of possibility in others.
- Leaders who show gratitude catalyze efficacy in others.
- Leaders who express hope increase motivation in others.
- Leaders who resist nostalgia help people express new visions.
- Leaders who express confidence invite others to learn.
- Leaders who authentically comfort others help them to listen to and absorb information.
- Leaders who are compassionate help reduce isolation for others.

The ability to stay calm first requires heightened awareness of one's own urge to react with familiar emotional responses that may not, in fact, initiate the most helpful set of actions for bouncing forward. Leaders who stay calm mindfully regulate their emotions in order to produce helpful emotions and actions in others. Resilient leaders tend to look at each fresh crisis with interest as opposed to judgment. They are less likely to see trouble as catastrophes and are more likely to say things like "Well, isn't this interesting?" Perhaps they would even go so far as to allow they are in a fine kettle of fish. But they often do nothing, at least for a little while. When they do take action, it usually results in a good outcome with concern for others as well as for themselves.

Summary
When resilient leaders begin the cycle of Leadership Resilience in Action, they remain calm and alert, which sets an empowering emotional tone for others to follow.

Activities and Questions

1. With a particular challenge from your leadership work in mind, and as you reflect on the content in this chapter, what will you draw from the leadership resilience-enabling capacities of Relationships, Resonance, and Renewal, and how do you need to bolster them?

   The leadership challenge I'm thinking of is:

2. In order to help myself and others stay calm I need to draw on these ideas from the three leadership resilience enablers:

   • Relationships:

   • Resonance:

   • Renewal:

3. What would it feel like for you to actually have the strength to do nothing when what you really want to do is react?

4. Make a list of all the emotions you can think of, both helpful and destructive. Then, thinking of a specific leadership challenge either from the past or present, and write down the impact of that emotion, if you were to exhibit it, on the people you lead.

5. Practice resilience on the small losses you face every day in your personal and work life. For example, when you miss a green light, lose your cell phone, lock yourself out of the house, or get a flat tire on your bike in the middle of long ride. When you miss an important call, when others are late for a meeting you planned, when a deadline is moved up in your calendar, or when an additional piece of information is requested at the last minute. These frequent and annoying events, which are part and parcel to the daily churn of life, provide plenty of low-stake opportunities to practice and strengthen the cycle of resilience in action. Every time you respond resiliently, beginning with Stay Calm to these low-level disruptions, you retrain your brain for more resilience when the big disruptions occur.

6. For one week, make a note in your calendar, plan book, or journal whenever you feel upset or catch yourself saying something you later regret, as this is a visible signal that your fight-or-flight inclinations have compromised your resilience. Importantly, the faster you recover from a state of feeling hijacked by your emotions, the more resilient you are (Goleman, 2011; Davidson et al., 2003). With a friend, partner, or leadership coach, reflect on the event:

   • What were the triggers?

   • How long did it take you to recover?

   • Did you do anything specific to recover?

   • What were you aware of as it was happening?

   • How did it affect the next thing you had to do that day?

7. Ask yourself if your typical reaction or the way you feel like responding will move you closer to people and toward the vision of the organization. If it won't, count to 10 and then think of another option.

8. Pay attention to the positive events of the day. Most of us have many positive events every day, but because we don't reflect on them as much as we reflect on negative events, we don't benefit from the well-being they produce for us. Spend more time lingering in the memory of the positive events of each day.

9. Take a couple of breaths. Look at the bigger picture in addition to the scene right in front of you. Instead of responding negatively, actually say out loud: "Well, isn't that interesting."

10. Consider what would be the exact opposite of your usual reaction and try that first. See what happens.

11. Choose to be a leader. In other words, step up and resonate a demeanor that draws out the best in others.

12. Learn mindfulness, a technique you practice much like meditation, to train the brain to register and fully focus on events in the present moment, without reacting (Goleman, 2011). Mindfulness practice consists of sitting quietly for a period of time while focusing on your breath. When thoughts come to you, go ahead and notice them but then return your focus to your breath. Over time, the ability to resist impulsive reactions transfers to the workplace. You'll know you are getting good at this when you feel a reduction in your overall level of stress.

7

Carry On

St. Francis of Assisi was once asked what he would do if he knew he had only one more day to live. He said, "I would continue to hoe my garden."

- Stay Calm
- Reflect and Celebrate
- Carry On
- Leadership Resilience in Action
- Instigate Adaptive Action
- Accept the New Reality
- Want Something More

Reminder: As you read this chapter, note where the ideas and strategies presented draw on the leadership resilience-enabling capacities of relationships, resonance, and renewal. Then, at the end of the chapter, write down what you want to learn about or experience in order to bolster the capacities so that you are better able to respond in the aftermath of adversity and disruptive change.

On any given day, both positive and negative events, occurring in our own families, communities, and around the world, provide poignant backdrops for conversations about resilience. Round the clock media coverage bombards us with images of school shootings, hurricanes, and terrorism—the horrific details of course, but also stories of compassion and people pulling together (perhaps receiving less coverage but there all the same if we look for them). Meanwhile, within our own families and communities, we experience the neither unusual nor rare presence of loss in our lives. People we love grow old and die. We experience health challenges. We retire, move to new homes and friendships, and fortunes change. We take on new challenges at work, our kids grow up and move away and we anxiously watch them experience the struggles and joys of becoming adults. Whether they come through our own doing, are part of the cycle of life, or are caused by external forces mostly out of our control, these "disorienting dilemmas," as Jack Mezirow so wonderfully calls them (2000), catalyze growth for us. When it comes right down to it, we wouldn't have it any other way.

Maintain Momentum

Nuanced within the disorienting dilemmas of life, we find the seeds of leadership resilience in action. One particularly admirable characteristic of leadership resilience is the ability to carry on—to continue to show up and do the hard work of the day, to maintain momentum within the organization, even when it seems like everything is coming apart around us.

Perhaps the only thing more unsettling than disruptive change is realizing that while your attention and energy was diverted, the rest of the organization fell apart. A practical illustration of how people outside the workplace help each other carry on can be seen in families and neighborhoods after someone passes away. People tend to rally around the bereaved family to bring food, to take out the garbage, walk the dog, and throw in a load of laundry. Instinctively, after a loss we know that common yet important routines still need attention. To let them go would only intensify the process of grieving and recovery. These simple and ordinary tasks sustain the momentum of life. They facilitate our personal resilience by keeping us moving forward into the next day, and the next day, and the next day. Their familiarity provides comfort and a sense of hope. Tomorrow is a new day.

Sustain Organizational Operations

In the aftermath of adversity, leaders cannot afford to allow routines to stall, as this only compounds disruption and makes stepping forward into the new reality that much more difficult. While in the raw stage of change and loss, the routines that maintain organizational operations also sustain momentum for the organization. In the context of Leadership Resilience in Action, to Carry On means leaders must see to the operations of the organization, to keep things running where they can and where they must. In healthcare settings, no matter what else has happened, safety procedures must still function without interruption, patient care needs to be at the highest standards, and resources must be provided to support the nursing staff.

Ask for Help

Resilient leaders have cultivated a robust network of diverse relationships, poised to help them when needed. When it comes to sustaining the momentum of the organization, asking for their help is a wise move. But it may be difficult for nurse leaders to ask for what they need. Marjorie Barter, a nurse leader in California who is also a Vietnam veteran says, "Sometimes what doesn't kill you temporarily makes you weaker. Because most nurses and nurse leaders project resilience as an expectation of the job, we don't seek the kind of help we could be seeking."

Referring to the role nurse leaders play in creating a climate where front-line nurses feel comfortable asking for help, CNO Richard Billingsley says,

> *Because nurses are the caregivers, they forbid themselves from asking for care for themselves--asking for care means we are weak and we don't want to be weak. As leaders, we need to let front-line staff know they can ask for what they need.*

Richard adds, "When I was a staff nurse and a patient of mine died, I cried. People around me considered this a negative. As a nurse leader, I need to let people know it is OK."

Katherine Bullard, a nurse leader from California, shares her experience:

> *I was in San Antonio at the time of Hurricane Ike and observed what happened as we received patients who were evacuated from the coast. I saw that we expect a high level of stamina from nurses and when they don't show extreme strength, we think they are not living up to expectations. We forget that people also need time to grieve.*

But asking for help should not be limited to times of crisis and tragedy. The beauty of asking for help is that when it is given and received, important relationships become stronger and resilience increases.

Giving and Gratitude

Asking for help is a reciprocal proposition with benefits to the giver and receiver alike. When you ask for what you need, you get better at asking for what you need—something many leaders are not good at doing. In addition, you experience the emotion of gratitude, which is a source of renewal and energy. Simultaneously, the other parties gain the experience of giving, which increases compassion and increases their sense of well-being.

Mitigate Suffering for Others

In order to carry on in the aftermath of adversity, leaders sometimes have to take steps to release people from what they believe is holding them back. Most people are stronger than they believe they are, but for some, acute situations or a compounded number of disruptive events can push them to the edges of their resilience. To illustrate this point, understanding an engineering term known as the modulus of resilience is key. The modulus of resilience describes the extent to which solid structures, such as steel beams, can bend without becoming permanently deformed. Although steel beams that shore up skyscrapers are very strong, they also flex a little within an acceptable range without becoming damaged. When the range is exceeded, however, even steel will snap. Some people do too. In the midst of disruptive change, you can make it easier for people to eventually bounce forward by taking steps to mitigate the pain of change.

Resistance: Signals of Low Resilience

In organizations, people usually display the limits of their resilience by resisting change. Sadly, their resistance holds them back from participating in emerging opportunities and limits their professional and personal experiences—the very conditions that catalyze resilience and make work and life interesting. Resilient leaders care about their less resilient colleagues, and they look for ways to mitigate their discomfort without compromising the forward motion of the organization. Nurse leader Megan Damon describes it this way: "We have to reduce the burden without reducing the goal."

The symptoms of resistance are usually visible: people complain, disengage, miss meetings, withhold requested information, or they simply ignore responsibilities. These symptoms of resistance signal a fragile state of resilience. Rather than focus on the symptoms, however, leaders need to understand that mitigation has much to do with responding swiftly and appropriately to the emotional needs of the people involved (Tedlow, 2010). In complex organizations, for example, emotional needs include fears of incompetency in the unknown future state, stress over loss of favored resources, sadness about losing key relationships, and anxiety over incomplete information or misinformation.

At the root of these emotions is loss of attachment: the state of emotional distress experienced by people when the structures or people or cultures they have come to lean on for support disappear (Grady & Grady, 2012). Writing about organizational change in general, Grady and Grady suggest that substitutions for what was lost help people regain a sense of stability as they ease into change. They write that, "those replacements could be a leader, a favored object, a method of communication, a continuing education series, a technology, a colleague, a culture, or any combination of these items" (p. 86). Minnesota nurse leader Megan Damon says,

> *Some people need to understand every aspect of the change—they want to read every peer review article they can in order to be able to move forward comfortably. Others want a short and sweet bulletin. So you have to provide that background information and be physically present to help them process the information.*

Maslow's Hierarchy: A Mitigation Framework

Maslow's theory of motivation, presented in his famous hierarchy of needs, also offers insight about how leaders can mitigate the negative effects of disruptive change for the people they lead.

Maslow, who was influential in management research starting in the 1940s, put forth the idea that people have fundamental needs, experienced in a hierarchy of priorities. These needs are represented in a pyramid that includes physiological requirements and safety at the bottom levels, love and belonging at the mid-level, and self-esteem, self-actualization, and self-transcendence at the higher levels (Koltko-Rivera, 2006).

According to the theory, individuals are highly motivated to do whatever it takes to pursue and obtain resources to satisfy their needs at high-priority unfulfilled levels found at the bottom of the pyramid, such as food, water, shelter, and feeling loved or belonging to a group. The theory holds that until lower level needs are fulfilled, people are unmotivated to engage in higher level needs where we find achievement, respect, creativity, problem solving, and serving a greater good.

Unexpected change and adversity may jeopardize previously met motivational needs, causing employees to focus on satisfying basic needs and to disengage from contributing to organizational goals. During times of adversity and disruptive change, Maslow's hierarchy can be an effective tool for assessing what people need to be more resilient.

For example, during and after Hurricane Ike, Nan Ybarra, a Texas nurse leader (to whom you were introduced in a previous chapter), describes what she did to support affected staff:

> *Several employees lost their homes and quite a few were suffering from post-traumatic stress. I contacted all the employees who still had PTO (professional time off) in their bank, and organized a drive where they could donate them to colleagues who needed time to get their lives back in order. There were some people who lost everything. So we also set up a wish list of necessary items that we bought for them and we purchased toys for their children.*

Helping nurses regain footing at lower levels of Maslow's hierarchy, as Nan did after Hurricane Ike, is absolutely crucial. In natural disasters, uncertainties about the wellness of loved ones, not to mention loss of basic needs such as fresh water and shelter, preoccupy everyone. But nurse leaders can also use the hierarchy to satisfy higher needs for individuals. Examples of how resilient leaders mitigate discomfort for the nurses they lead abound. Minnesota nurse leader Marcia McCormick explains:

Sometimes what people need to do is vent. They just need to say what they have to say, and then they feel better. Even if at first they think I'm going to magically solve their complaints, they learn that I don't. I just listen. Then, we move on.

Another example of mitigation comes from nurse leader Megan Damon, also from Minnesota, who says, "I see myself as a 'barrier remover' to whatever prevents nurses from being autonomous clinicians and professional nurses."

Writing about the relationship between healthy work environments and nurse engagement and retention, authors Lisa Groff Paris and Mary Terhaar say of using Maslow's hierarchy, "Once nurses' basic needs are met, their focus will shift toward achieving higher level needs, including their sense of belonging, self-esteem, and self-actualization" (2010).

Also writing about nurse retention, in her article *Keep that Nurse* that appears on the website WorkingNurse.com, Geneviève M. Clavreul (2014) where the remarks on how some hospitals focus only on pay and tangible incentives to motivate nurses and improve morale, Clavreul says that money, though important, isn't everything. She writes:

Instead, it may be that the need to participate, be recognized, be creative, and to experience a sense of worth are better motivators in an affluent society, where many have already achieved an acceptable measure of freedom from hunger and threats to security and personal safety, and are now driven by higher-order psychological needs. (paragraph 9)

Maslow's framework provides nurse leaders with an extra tool for identifying ways to mitigate the pain of adversity. By paying attention to both the lower order and higher order needs of nurses (such as involving the nursing staff in designing creative recovery strategies, assuring they have control over their nursing practice, and providing a culture of teamwork and collaboration), a nurse leader has a powerful set of strategies to facilitate bouncing forward for individuals and as a result, for the organization.

Ways Resilient Leaders Mitigate the Losses Inherent in Disruptive Change
Leaders that take action to lessen the harshness and intensity of pain that accompanies disruptive change have a keen sensitivity to the modulus of

resilience in others, which makes bouncing forward much easier for everyone. Here are a few helpful ideas:

- Be active and visible in your leadership. Walk around, talk to people, and listen well.
- Spontaneously jump in and work alongside people.
- Provide focused professional development so people can develop needed new skills to be successful in the new reality.
- Communicate timely, accurate, and frequent information, even if it is only to say that new information is unavailable.
- Assure that front-line leaders are not negatively focusing on what has been lost but are advocates for forward motion.
- Give solace and comfort. Sit and listen to people who are most impacted or most invested in what was lost.
- Use humor respectfully. One leader put a big jar of coins in the staff break room with a note that said, "Afraid of change? Leave yours here!"
- Involve people in designing and trying out new forward pathways.
- Help people see their role in the new reality and support them in connecting their new roles with their passions.
- Reduce low-priority demands—take things off their plate where you can.
- Connect people with each other for mentoring, coaching, and friendships.

Summary

In the immediate aftermath of disruptive change, resilient leaders make sure that the organization continues to function. Doing so sustains momentum and makes it easier for people to bounce forward. In order to Carry On, leaders call on their network of relationships for support, and they take steps to mitigate the pain of change for others.

Activities and Questions

1. With a particular challenge from your leadership work in mind, and as you reflect on the content in this chapter, what will you draw from the leadership resilience-enabling capacities of Relationships, Resonance, and Renewal, and how do you need to bolster them?

   The leadership challenge I'm thinking of is:

2. In order to help myself and others Carry On, I need to draw on these ideas
    from the three leadership resilience-enabling capabilities:

    *   Relationships:

    *   Resonance:

    *   Renewal:

3. With one or more specific challenges in mind, who do you want to ask for
    help? How can you reciprocate?

4. What functions within the organization and your department run smoothly?
    Which ones do not function well unless they have a lot of guidance and
    oversight? Build in redundancies now to keep the more needy functions
    operating smoothly in the event of disruptive change.

5. Who has the skills needed to jump in and cover for other colleagues as
    needed? Where do you have helpful redundancies in skills, people, and
    resources?

6. Thinking of the people you work with, what do they value during times of
    change? Go back and read the section in this chapter titled "Ways Resilient
    Leaders Mitigate the Losses of Disruptive Change" and identify several
    strategies that fit your culture.

8

Accept the New Reality

The beginning of wisdom is to call things by their right names.

—Chinese proverb

Reminder: As you read this chapter, note where the ideas and strategies presented draw on the leadership resilience-enabling capacities of relationships, resonance, and renewal. Then, at the end of the chapter, write down what you want to learn about or experience in order to bolster the capacities so that you are better able to respond in the aftermath of adversity and disruptive change.

At some point, in response to disruptive change, resilient leaders take the first visible steps into the new reality and they must beckon others to come along. The new reality includes the social, emotional, political, cultural, professional, and personal facets and forces, both negative and positive, that come into view when the smoke begins to clear. Many people find the prospect of stepping into the unknown territory of new realities terribly frightening. Leaders are not exempt from feelings of fear and anxiety, but resilient leaders understand that debilitating emotions and fear-driven perceptions prevent them from seeing the opportunity in change, and in meeting their leadership responsibilities.

Adjust Your Perspective

New realities require leaders to think accurately about the implications of adversity—about what will happen from this point forward into the foreseeable future (Reivich & Shatté, 2002). The ability to de-escalate adversities by adjusting and revising your perspective in order to think accurately is a sure sign of resilience. While reframing one's perspective promotes individual resilience, leaders have the extra requirement of helping others see clearly yet optimistically toward a future they will need to create.

Consider the story of Lee, a novice charge nurse who is low in leadership resilience. Lee tends to perceive disruptive change as an indictment against his leadership style. He takes everything personally and blows up easily. The nurses on his shift whisper among themselves that he has a short fuse. Lee's underlying assumption is that disruption of any sort reflects poorly on him. Moreover, he projects this assumption onto others, believing that they also attribute disruptive changes in the environment to his flagging leadership skills. As a result, Lee comes off as defensive and he misses many opportunities to transform adversity into growth.

For example, when the staff climate survey revealed low marks in the domain of communication, Lee told his supervisor "The only reason these nurses say communication is a problem is because they don't like some of the things I have to tell them need to change. As usual, they are shooting the messenger." Laboring under this skewed perspective, Lee began to visibly withdraw from talking with the nursing staff at all. Ironically, Lee creates most of the mischief he later feels he has to defend.

Lee's response is decidedly uncharacteristic of leadership resilience. If he were able to reframe his perspective, Lee would see that most of the information that disrupts his equilibrium and causes him to react defensively is not about him personally, but is instead helpful feedback signaling opportunity to improve. Let's take a look at some of the many ways Lee could more positively reframe his perspective about the climate survey:

1. I am fortunate the nurses on my team responded to the climate survey. This means they value communication.
2. Two-way communication is an important variable for patient outcomes. I'm eager to learn new ways to accomplish this, which, after all, is our purpose.
3. Our nurses value communication with the leadership team because it allows them to concentrate on their nursing practice..
4. We conduct community surveys in order to improve our practices. We value and respect all responses and can learn from each and every responder.

Equipped with any one of the reframed perspectives above, Lee would have a variety of leadership responses at his disposal that elude him under his current paradigm. Instead of responding with disrespect and disdain (not qualities of leadership), Lee would extend gratitude, seek innovative ideas, set an example for front-line nurses, and make changes that could have a profound effect on patient outcomes.

Contrast Lee's story with that of Sharon Rorhback, founder of Nurses for Newborns. When the non-profit organization was in its tenth year, Sharon was surprised to discover they only had about two weeks' worth of operating funds in the bank. Apparently, a calculation error was made and no one knew that funds were seriously low. Sharon immediately took a pay cut and began appealing to regular donors for financial assistance. One donor made a substantial contribution with the stipulation that they meet regularly with Sharon and her leadership team, like a kitchen cabinet and help Nurses for Newborns put in safeguards and processes to sustain a healthy budget from this point forward. Some leaders would have rankled at being told they needed to accept an advisory group in order to receive the generous donation needed to continue operations, but not Sharon. She explains:

> *I welcomed the opportunity to work with this smart group who wanted to help us and it was so gratifying to build the infrastructure for future financial management. By the time I retired, we had a budget of 4.5 million dollars all paid through grants, donors, and fund raisers.*

Sharon's ability to perceive the kitchen cabinet proviso as an advantage and a welcomed force to make Nurses for Newborns more resilient in the future underscores just how powerfully a leader's perspective affects the people they lead. Sharon says:

> *The leader has to portray adversity as opportunity and they must convey this with a high level of confidence. You have to change the lens that people are looking through in a convincing way—you have to really see things differently yourself then others will trust you and will begin to see possibilities. This is the start of innovation.*

When it comes to accepting the new reality and setting the stage for positive action, leaders who reframe unhelpful and maladaptive perspectives change the trajectory of events to follow. As Seligman (1991) puts it, "Our thoughts are not merely reactions to events; they change what ensues" (p. 7). Realizing that thoughts and reactions create the future could make leaders hesitant in making decisions; what if we do the wrong thing? You can mitigate this concern for yourself by examining your perspective to see how it is driving your actions. If your perspective about any given situation includes blaming others or shunning responsibility, you can alter it. You can access your highest values and align your perspectives with them. When your perspectives are guided by your highest values, you can make decisions more quickly and then move on.

Reflecting on how leaders overcome negative and unhelpful perspectives, Sharon Rorhbach emphasizes:

> *As a leader you really have to model the way and you also have to shepherd other people. This is harder after a crisis than it is during regular times of leadership. The characteristic you need is self-confidence. Therefore, you have to overcome fear of failure.*

Front-line nurse leader Stephanie Youngberg has keen personal insight about the challenge of overcoming fear. She says:

> I have a hard time forgiving myself because I hold myself to such high standards. I never want to do the wrong thing for patients of course, and I don't want to fail. But I also know that when I'm working to my full capacity, I can't do everything perfectly all the time—not when you need to make fast decisions and when **not** making a fast, good decision would be the wrong thing.

Understanding that fear often paralyzes action, resilient leaders work hard to cultivate trust—trust in themselves and in others. In their article "Mindfulness, Hope and Compassion: A Leader's Road Map to Renewal" (2006), McKee, Johnston, and Massimilian say that trust increases when leaders are mindful enough to ask themselves questions about their behavior that put them in touch with the "subtle messages" of the people they lead—questions such as "Am I acting in concert with my values? Am I the leader I aspire to be? How am I doing managing the stress of my current situation? How are my key people feeling these days" (p. 3). Ultimately trust diminishes fear, which in turn reduces the stress that makes leaders negative, dissonant, and withdrawn.

Resist Nostalgia

Disruptive change is not only unexpected, but more importantly, it is change—and as everyone knows, even planned change can be troublesome. Change thrusts people into transition—that disorienting space between the known and unknown (Bridges, 1980) where the old rules, assumptions, and algorithms for "how we do things around here" no longer apply. This is a shaky time for some people, and nostalgia for what was lost will tug mightily at their hearts. Less resilient leaders rail against change. Oddly enough, they do so even when what they had before the change also caused them dismay. Leaders who glamorize the past or denigrate the potential of the new reality hold their colleagues and the organization back. As University of San Francisco's School of Nursing Dean, Judith Karshmer, observes, "As leaders we have to stop talking about how hard change is—the truth is that keeping the status quo is what is difficult."

Resistance to change is a symptom of nostalgia, and nostalgia undermines resilience. Referring to the move to create a national health insurance, nurse leader Shannon Nell, who is director of nursing and nursing education in Sandton, South Africa, says:

> *To overcome the pull of the past, you need to confront those colleagues whose typical response is to say, 'yes, but' to every change. You have to ask them to consider the consequences if we don't move forward with positive change for the greatest number of people.*

Confronting colleagues who want to hold on to obsolete traditions of the past takes courage. Leaders taking others into a new future cannot indulge in debilitating longing for the past. In fact, they must actively challenge organizational structures that work to preserve the past and therefore work against acceptance of the new reality. Not to do so sustains cultures that are toxic to new realities. Consider, for example, the glaring mismatch between vision and culture in wellness organizations that say they want a safe and healthy workforce but then continue to approve double shifts and unsafe staffing levels.

Resisting Nostalgia

Peter Drucker is known to have said, "culture eats strategy for breakfast." This means that even as leaders seek pathways forward into new realities, they must simultaneously help the culture evolve coherently to support the change. Resilient leaders can begin this challenging work by engaging others in reviewing existing policies and past decisions, and reshaping or excising those that no longer apply (Hamel, 2009). Nurse leader Marcia McCormick says, "The secret of change is focusing all your energy on the new instead of the old."

Resilient leaders resist nostalgia by describing the new reality in present tense and vivid detail, taking care to identify what still exists from the past and what is new and good. These details are new bearings; they help people find their way, and they give them stability and courage to respond. For example, over the years, the patients in several mental health programs where Marcia McCormick is a director experience not only more serious forms of mental illness, but they often also have many other serious medical issues. Marcia says:

> *Some nurses are very nostalgic about the way it used to be. I have to help them understand that we are not going to get 'better patients.' I've set up*

a grieving process and a wishing process to help with this. I make myself available to listen, to let them vent for a while, but then I bring them back to figuring out how to make things work.

At no time is accepting new realities more important than when disruptive events make their way into the newspapers, on television, and on the Internet. Many times, what the media considers newsworthy are comments the leader has no control over, such as those made by board members, the families of patients, other healthcare workers, and patients themselves. One leader, whose hospital was at the center of controversy when an inpatient left the building unnoticed and was later found deceased a few blocks away, has the following advice:

Under these circumstances do not deviate from the mission. When you are clear on the details, it is important to be honest about whatever happened and then pull people together and let the mission guide you toward the best response.

Nurse leader Tarina Kwong says it is important for new nurse leaders especially to look around and seek the perspective of colleagues who have lead through multiple changes. Tarina says, "I work with a nurse who is 71 years old—she was born at my hospital! She has seen so many changes and is still passionate about the profession." Tarina adds:

I've had the opportunity to visit nurses in China every year, and I see that they do not have the chance to change their roles within nursing the way we do here in the United States. As a result, they often lose their passion for nursing. Nurses who have experienced a lot of change have so much to offer.

Summary

Resilient leaders step confidently in the new realities that emerge in the aftermath of disruptive change. These leaders are adept at adjusting their perspective in order to see the opportunities in adversity and in resisting the powerful force of nostalgia. They are especially vigilant about resisting the temptation to let nostalgia for the past creep into their conversations with others. Instead, they bring their absorbed insights from the past forward, and they apprehend new realities through fresh eyes.

Activities and Questions

1. With a particular challenge from your leadership work in mind, and as you reflect on the content in this chapter, what will you draw from the leadership resilience-enabling capacities of Relationships, Resonance, and Renewal, and how do you need to bolster them?

   The leadership challenge I'm thinking of is:

2. In order to help myself and others to Accept the New Reality, I need to draw on these ideas from the three leadership resilience-enabling capacities:

   • Relationships:

   • Resonance:

   • Renewal:

3. What do you say to yourself and what do you hear others say that signify a nostalgic view of the past?

4. What has been the good that has come to you from the last new reality you stepped into?

5. Who or what would give you courage in new realities?

6. What do you want to learn in order to improve your framing and reframing skills in the face of your leadership challenges?

9

Want Something More

Start something that matters.

—Blake Mycoskie (2011)

> *Reminder:* As you read this chapter, note where the ideas and strategies presented draw on the leadership resilience-enabling capacities of relationships, resonance, and renewal. Then, at the end of the chapter, write down what you want to learn about or experience in order to bolster your capacities so you are better able to respond in the aftermath of adversity and disruptive change.

As people begin to accept new realities, they enter an intriguing phase of creating a future that leverages the opportunities—the silver linings of disruptive change.

I (Elle) will give you a personal example: While I was working on another writing project, my computer crashed and my files were unrecoverable. To add insult to injury, I had not set up my backup drive properly. As a researcher, writer, and small-business owner, this means I lost an enormous amount of intellectual property. More than a year's worth of writing and work disappeared into thin air. There was nothing left for me to do but recreate the book that was due in four weeks, and begin to develop from scratch everything I needed to do my research and work. At first losing my files felt like a horrible tragedy. But as I started to strategize my recovery, I had this incredible insight: Even though I had evolved as a researcher, writer, businessperson, and leader, for the sake of efficiency, I relied on old tools, forms, processes, and policies that did not reflect my growth. In other words, for the sake of efficiency, I was settling for mediocrity. Until the tragedy of my computer crash, I might not have taken time to update and transform the way I do my work.

Another example from the world of nursing comes from a novice nurse named Annie, whose mentor Carol (Annie and Carol are pseudonyms) suffered a massive heart attack while at home on her day off, and died alone. In life, Carol had been a champion for nurse wellness and was very concerned about the stress many nurses were under on the job. She participated on committees to help improve workplace conditions and she always spoke up when she felt that nurse wellness was at risk. The fact that she died of a heart attack struck Annie as especially poignant. Feeling bewildered, sad, and overwhelmed, this young nurse was determined to make something good come out of the loss of her beloved mentor. She did not want Carol's death to be in vain. Annie looked around the department and picked the one thing she could do immediately to help increase wellness for other nurses: she organized the supply cabinets. When Annie saw that this one small act helped to alleviate some of the stress in her department, she began to wonder what more could be done to create safe and wellness promoting physical spaces, for nurses and patients alike. When the hospital established a committee to design a new wing, and issued an open invitation to nurses to contribute innovative design ideas, Annie readily joined in. Annie said, "We lost Carol, but we did not lose her ideals. This is an opportunity for Carol's death to mean something, to make the future better for other nurses."

Want Something More

The losses that make resilience possible also provide the necessary breakdowns that press leaders to imagine new potentials within themselves and the system. Resilient leaders have a knack for helping people emerge from difficulties yearning for something more—a knack that begins with modeling a demeanor of openness. Judy Karshmer, who is dean of the University of San Francisco's School of Nursing, puts it this way: "The moment you say 'no,' you teach others around you that they are not up to the challenges that come their way. Instead, you need to say 'yes' to whatever comes up and then turn it into an opportunity."

This phase in the Leadership Resilience in Action Cycle is called Want Something More. In this phase, the hope of transformation takes over. During this phase, highly resilient leaders continue to absorb new information about the changes around them in the present moment, while they also stream their energy toward designing a better future. Want Something More is characterized by a sense of possibility. When I lost my computer data for example, I began to think, *Well, now that I have to get a new computer anyhow, why don't I get the MacBook Air that I've been coveting? And isn't now the perfect time to invest in Dropbox to back up files for the whole family? And now, why don't I load that new project management software?*

In complex organizations, resilient leaders yearn to transform adversity into growth, to torque loss into change. While in this phase, they ask questions to cast their thoughts and the thoughts of the people they lead, toward designing the future. These questions are both evocative and provocative—they draw on emotions and they are action-oriented. Examples include:

1. What does this loss now make possible? What does it take off our plate and clear out of our way?
2. What do I/we feel passionate about?
3. How can I/we use the highest ideals of our mission to guide us now?
4. How do I/we give opportunities to others as we move forward?

5. What solutions actually solve long-standing, vexing problems?

6. What can I/we do now that mobilizes the best evidence-based practice?

7. Where can I/we lead?

8. How do we assure that the most vulnerable of our stakeholders benefit from what I/we do next?

9. How do I/we sustain our best effort now in order to make the future better for others?

Play A Bigger Game

Sometimes, as seen in the story of Anne and the disorganized supply cabinet, adversity reveals inadequacies that up until this point have been easier to live with than do something about. But in the aftermath of loss, when resilient leaders have a chance to create the future, they challenge themselves to go big, to up the ante and play a bigger game. And why not? Adversity has a way of showing you where you may have been leading small, where you have not been stepping up to have a wider, deeper, more sustainable impact on people and the system.

Highly resilient nurse leaders don't wait for adversity in order to find ways to play a bigger game. They learn to gain the "upsides of creative destruction" (Homer-Dixon, 2006) by thinking bigger about thriving initiatives. For example, Sharon Rohrbach from Nurses for Newborns invited nursing, medical, and law students from local universities to accompany nurses on their home visits to new moms and babies. Sharon says:

> *My intention was to show them what it is like to be poor and to need help. I wanted them to remember the experience when they rise to places of power and influence in their professional lives. Many of these students became committed to our programs and eventually served on the board, joined committees, became donors, and helped with fundraisers. This helped our newborns of course but it also is a way to improve society.*

Ask Thoughtful Leadership Questions (TLQs)

In the context of leadership resilience, wanting something more requires people to move toward new realities that challenge the previous status quo. This is the time in the change process when people recognize they have a voice in creating the new or polished organizational vision and the pathways forward. At this point, resilient leaders ask powerful questions that get people talking about the possibilities they see in the aftermath of disruptive change.

Ways to Up the Ante and Play a Bigger Game

- Arrange for novice nurses to view quality nursing practice. Invite emerging and developing nurse leaders to shadow you for a day or more.

- Write and speak about your leadership work (new perspectives, new applications of common perspectives, ideas that may be contrary to conventional wisdom, new tools) in order to contribute to the knowledge base of others.

- Take an effective initiative already in place to a deeper level of implementation.

- Reengineer a cumbersome process so people can achieve results more efficiently and with less stress.

- Build partnerships where none currently exist.

- Apply knowledge and skills to a new problem or in a new way.

- Show the coherence of your work to the work of others in the organization.

- Share leadership responsibilities and delegate important outcomes to others.

- Add a teaching/mentoring/professional development component to an initiative or project you lead.

- Flow benefits from an initiative to the most vulnerable stakeholders.

- Support front-line nurse leaders by removing barriers and revising unhelpful policies.

- Apply an existing service, product, or process to create social justice.

- Collect stories to add to disaggregated data in order to build a full profile of information.

- Involve others in early experimentation, testing, and revision of new initiatives.

- Extend an existing initiative to include a new group of internal or external stakeholders.

"Thought leadership questions" is a term I (Elle) coined in my book *Renewal Coaching Fieldbook: How Effective Leaders Sustain Meaningful Change* (Allison et al., 2012). In the *Renewal Coaching Fieldbook*, I write that thoughtful leadership questions "elevate discussions between people in the organization away from habitual ways of thinking that lead to cliché ideas that rarely provide inspirational thought" (p. 18). In the aftermath of disruptive change, resilient leaders get together with people and ask questions that invite them to have a say in designing the future. Questions that either impose or remove limitations, called "constraining questions" (Dyer, Gregersen, & Christensen, 2011), provide you with a specific tool for encouraging people to imagine possibilities and take them beyond their fears.

Constraining Questions

Constraining questions are what-if questions that either impose or eliminate constraints as a way to catalyze innovation. To impose constraints, for example, ask questions like this: "What if we imposed a zero tolerance policy about team members who don't follow hand hygiene expectations?" Or "What if grant funding was withdrawn for this initiative—how would we still accomplish the goals of the program?" Or "What if this technology failed in a natural disaster—what else would we do to know that patients were stable?" Questions that eliminate constraints sound like this: "Let's imagine we didn't have strict policy about patient discharge routines—who would best decide when a patient was ready to go home?" Or "What if we suspended the practice of nurses caring only for the patients assigned to them—how could patient outcomes change?" Or "What if we were comfortable with post-operative patients emailing us once they returned home—how would that affect their recovery?"

Whether they impose or eliminate conditions, constraining questions have the unique ability to cast the mind toward exploration as opposed to limitations and, similar to brainstorming, they have a way of surfacing surprising ideas. When you ask constraining questions to encourage people in the organization to share their thoughts, feelings, and ideas with you after disruptive change, you invite them to have a voice in the re-visioning process.

Naturally, after you ask a question, you must fall to silence so people can respond. When you really listen, not only will you learn what the people you lead think is now possible in the organization, but as they hear themselves speak, they will learn about themselves. As they hear the ideas they come up with in response to the constraining questions you ask, they may be surprised to discover just how resilient and creative they are.

Just Listen

In the aftermath of adversity, the altered landscape of the organization often requires new decisions. Sometimes policies and procedures need to be revised. Other times resources need to be moved around and cultural practices about how people interact with each other need to change. In order to make new decisions, leaders certainly expose themselves to large quantities of data, evidence, and information, which they use well in the decision-making process. But resilient leaders go a step further: They listen to the stories people tell about what they personally need in order to bounce forward. Stories go above and beyond hard facts and reveal the heart as well as the mind. Story collections illuminate the field surrounding decisions, making clear the best course of action (Allison et al., 2012). The listening required to attend to these stories is based in discipline and compassion (Nichols, 1995).

Kim Klein, who is a leader in nonprofit work in the Bay Area sees listening as being key to achieving buy-in: "People don't form opinions if no one asks them what they think and listens to them. They have to hear their own voice and then see if they like themselves—if what they hear themselves say out loud really is what they feel" (Allison, 2012, p. 171).

An Underrated Leadership Skill

Listening is an underrated leadership skill; everyone thinks they are already listening experts so they do not prioritize learning how to listen well. What prevents leaders from listening? Some leaders believe that unless they are dispensing wisdom, advice, and opinions, they are not doing their job. Other leaders fear wrong-headed ideas will prevail unless their voices dominate conversations. These leaders are well-meaning—they use their words to demonstrate leadership, and certainly, words matter. However, powerful words that inspire colleagues arise from listening longer and deeper than what is usual and even comfortable.

In the aftermath of disruptive change, listening is a critical tool that resilient leaders use to help people think out loud about what they want in the new reality. One leader puts it this way:

> *When you listen, you show that you are willing to put yourself out there and that you are listening because you want to take action that people have had a hand in guiding. This means that even if they don't agree with you 100%, they know you listened to their input and it helps them manage the turbulence they feel as you move forward.*

Listening in the aftermath of adversity signals a prelude to action. It begins to make clear the way forward.

Purpose and Vision

Shared visions draw people into the future and establish high levels of commitment. They are a powerful source of inspiration and hope. Especially during times of disruptive change, however, new decisions are called for—many of which affect the tactics and strategies in play to achieve the vision. Mark Bielang, who is a school superintendent, has good advice for all leaders, including nurse leaders.

> *When you keep the vision front and center you remind people that they want something more. Especially when we have to make tough decisions the vision helps us stay focused so we can make tough decisions that are also good decisions. The vision helps people move forward in developing ideas.*

Some adversities reach beyond the strategy level to alter the current organizational vision itself. Although they are relatively stable, organizational visions do change, often due to the disruption created when we learn a better way of accomplishing our goals. Think if you can, for example, back to the days when we were unaware that good hand hygiene could mostly eliminate healthcare-associated infections. Before we had overwhelming evidence of this fact, many healthcare providers opted not to wash their hands—they thought it slowed them down and therefore diminished their ability to care for patients. Back then, nary a healthcare facility hung posters about hand washing or installed sinks in conspicuous locations. Now that we know better, we operate under new assumptions.

Pervasive innovations in the world around us also alter visions. New technologies, for example, now make it possible for healthcare professionals to assess the health of patients in remote locations, and collaborate with those who are onsite to provide treatment and care.

In the long run, organizations that embrace changes to the vision are more sustainable than those that do not. Evolving visions keep healthcare organizations relevant and in touch with the changing needs of their communities. Resilient nurse leaders must become adept at articulating the evolution of the organizational vision and the interplay between evolving visions and strategies. Whether it strikes at the heart of the organization's vision or not, disruptive change requires leaders and others to open themselves to new possibilities. This is what keeps the vision renewed and relevant, and it is what ultimately sustains the organization.

Summary

In the aftermath of adversity or disruptive change, resilient leaders lead others to Want Something More. They elicit this perspective by playing a bigger game and by asking thought leadership questions, listening, and keeping the purpose and evolving vision of the organization front and center.

Activities and Questions

1. With a particular challenge from your leadership work in mind, and as you reflect on the content in this chapter, what will you draw from the leadership resilience-enabling capacities of Relationships, Resonance, and Renewal, and how do you need to bolster them?

   The leadership challenge I'm thinking of is:

2. In order to help myself and others Want Something More, I need to draw on these ideas from the three leadership resilience enablers:

   • Relationships:

   • Resonance:

   • Renewal:

3. Thinking of a particular challenge, adversity, or disruptive change currently facing you, write as many constraining thought leadership questions as you can about it. Once you produce your list of questions, make another list of the stakeholders who would benefit from reflecting on them. Try a few out and see what happens. Reflect on the process and the outcome with a colleague, your coach, or your leadership team.

4. How does the specific challenge or adversity you are thinking of operate on the current vision or the strategies toward the vision? Are they in alignment with the current vision? Where do the current challenges call assumptions into question? Meet with a thought partner who will listen as you flesh this out.

5. What are all the positive possibilities in the new reality, as you see them?

6. How does the current vision in your organization usually evolve? Does it emerge out of crisis? Out of external demands such as rules and regulations? Out of opportunities that come along?

10

Instigate Adaptive Action

I think one's feelings waste themselves in words; they ought all to be distilled into actions, and into actions which bring results.

—Florence Nightingale (Letter to Mary Clarke (1844), quoted by Sir Edward Tyas Cook in *The Life of Florence Nightingale* (1913).

Reminder: As you read this chapter, note where the ideas and strategies presented draw on the leadership resilience-enabling capacities of relationships, resonance, and renewal. Then, at the end of the chapter, write down what you want to learn about or experience in order to bolster your capacities so you are better able to respond in the aftermath of adversity and disruptive change.

In the near aftermath of adversity, action is what makes leadership resilience so extraordinary. Action is bouncing forward. Different from the relatively languorous run up to long-term strategic planning, disruptive change challenges leaders with a compressed amount of time to make a plan and take meaningful action. In these cases, resilient leaders have no other choice: If they want their organizations to bounce forward, they must Instigate Adaptive Action—action that produces valuable information about the best pathways forward.

Instigate Adaptive Action

Adaptive actions are not rash; they are coherent to the mission of the organization. But because they are born out of challenge and surprising change, they may be uncommon and are more likely to arise from your intuition and out of improvisation instead of a text book. Their real value is that even when they create imperfect results or even go awry, adaptive action creates information that gets you closer to what will work. As nurse leader Mary Lou DeNatale, a nurse educator from the University of San Francisco, says, "There are times when you have to do something even if it is wrong. You concentrate on the good that comes from it and you figure out what to do next."

Like taking baby steps, adaptive action helps people "find their feet" within new situations while they simultaneously discover new passions within themselves. For this reason, Rachelle Larsen, a nurse leader from Minnesota emphasizes the importance of listening to colleagues during times of change—even when what they seem to be doing is venting. Rachelle says,

> Some people vent for a long time, and at first it seems so one-sided; they seem to presenting a narrow point of view. But when I listen, I eventually recognize how we can move forward with something that matters to this person.

Marjorie Barter, a nurse leader from California, looks at the process as a journey. She says, "Taking the long view is crucial to nurse leadership resilience. Yes, we see the next part of the road, but we also see where the whole road can possibly go." Nan Ybarro adds, "You have to be comfortable with uncertainty."

Leadership specialist Ron Heifetz (1998) makes a distinction between adaptive leadership and technical work. Technical work is evident when there are easily identifiable solutions where data is often used to guide decision-making and goal achievement related to strategic plans. In contrast, adaptive leadership requires uncovering the values and beliefs of people involved in change efforts and is required when there is a clash between values and beliefs, and coordinated action. Adaptive action also contributes to system learning. Daniel Kim (1991) suggests that organizational learning is directly related to the degree that people understand and appreciate the interaction and effects of quality relationships, quality communications, and quality of coordinated action in an organization.

In this phase of the Leadership Resilience Cycle, resilient leaders orchestrate the excitement and passion of the people they lead—especially those first followers who get behind good ideas, willingly try them out, adapt and improve them in the moment, and show others how to join in (Seivers, 2010). These enthusiastic individuals are indispensable to resilient leaders and to resilient organizations because they work out the kinks of new ideas, and take some of the pain out of the change process for the second wave of followers. They create momentum and buy in, making bouncing forward a reality.

Start Something

The authors of the book *The Innovator's DNA: Mastering the Five Skills of Disruptive Innovators*, Dyer, Gregersen, & Christensen (2011), write about the lack of information available to leaders after disruptive change and when they are making decisions about how to respond. They write, "Often the only way to get the necessary data to move forward is to run the experiment" (Kindle location 1883).

These ideas are central to those of Donald Schon, the highly regarded expert in organizational learning, who wrote about what it means to be a reflective practitioner. Describing the process of reflection in action, Schon writes in his seminal book, *The Reflective Practitioner: How Professionals Think in Action* (1983), "He [sic] carries out an experiment which serves to generate both a new understanding of the phenomenon and a change in the situation" (p. 68).

Resilient leaders believe disruptive change stimulates innovation, and they support those who feel moved to design experiences that create insight. As Dean Melnyk says, "I look for people with a twinkle in their eye and a fire in their belly." The nurses Dean Melnyk describes are those who suggest strategies and practices because they think they will make a difference. These are the nurses who can influence others and can help to bring innovations to scale to help even more patients and communities.

Inspired thought often arises, quite surprisingly, out of disruptive change and loss. In truth, leaders of complex systems never have as much control over how change will affect the organization as they think they do. Resilient leaders understand that the only way to really know how the system will function after you modify it is to modify it! Then observe what happens and use the resulting data to make mid-course corrections. Decide what to remain committed to, what to hone, what to cull, and then refine the new approaches that emerge.

Adaptive actions can be the start of something big—a new program, practice, or process. Other adaptive actions are subtle but still produce information that may reveal the next step. Here are a few examples of subtle adaptive actions resilient leaders instigate not long after disruptive change. Notice that each of these examples naturally produce information that get the ball rolling and could lead to excellent solutions:

- Examine and revise or remove unhelpful policies that prevent people from experimenting and taking risks.
- Make adaptations to the environment to create the conditions for success (physical space, time, people, and tools).
- Utilize different people and people in various fields for their ideas, resources, and talents.
- Remove rules and customs that prevent people from contributing.
- Introduce experiences that help people learn something difficult and crucial.
- Design a work around (a strategy to compensate or mitigate a cumbersome process) and show others how to use it.
- Examine and question assumptions (your own and those in the culture) that sustain beliefs about how things need to be done.

Stare Back at Fear

Needless to say, courageous experimentation is daunting in organizations where the prevailing culture punishes mistakes. Cultures intolerant of mistakes raise leaders who are paralyzed by the thought of taking action that may not lead to the ultimate solution. What if they lead in the wrong direction? Ironically, in the absence of action and reflection on results, leaders have nothing to go on; they cannot correct a course they have not yet begun. When it comes to leading with resilience, pockets of spontaneous experimentation in the aftermath of loss make a lot of sense. Dean Melnyk says "You have to keep the dream bigger than your fears, bigger than uncertainty. You have to persist. So many leaders get worn down and they give up right before whatever is going to sprout, comes up."

Sandra Gregg, a nurse leader from Oregon, suggests that nurses have many opportunities to face and conquer fear of failure when they take advantage of the many new careers and roles within nursing that are available to them. Sandra says, "For nurses who want to grow they have many opportunities to do so. At the same time, they are assured of a certain amount of stability when these opportunities are grounded in roles that are very patient- and family-centered." Just Culture, a movement that helps to improve decision-making, personal accountability, and organizational learning within high-risk fields such as health care and aviation, offers concepts and practices that promote a more fearless culture where nurses are encouraged to stretch themselves as Sandra describes. Just Culture calls for fair and just responses to employee errors by recognizing first that some mistakes arise out of faulty systems—not out of at risk or reckless behavior. The Just Culture movement, therefore, holds employees blameless for errors that occur as a result of system failure. This quality provides a hospitable climate that encourages employees to self-report errors, and allows the organization to learn from those errors (see ANA position statement, http://nursingworld.org/psjustculture).

Megan Damon, a nurse leader from Minnesota, tells a great story of instigating adaptive action, and of nurturing a culture where nurses are not afraid to try things. When a patient satisfaction survey revealed dissatisfaction with the noise decibel at night, Megan and her colleagues put their heads together to solve the problem. While Megan went about squirting oil on squeaky door hinges to make the environment quiet, one of the staff nurses suggested they concentrate on strategies other than using medications to help patients get to sleep. If patients were asleep, she said, they would not be aware of noises. Knowing that sleep engenders the healing process for patients, Megan found this idea to contain a great amount of practical wisdom. Megan says, "This nurse came up with the surprising and wonderful idea of a 'comfort menu' where patients could choose a healing sleep aid—lavender, guided imaging, ear plugs, a hand massage—whatever they thought would help them get to sleep." Megan wasn't worried if some nurses questioned the value of the comfort menu. She says, "We just had to go back to the patient satisfaction survey and look at the data. With the comfort menu, were patients sleeping better and more satisfied?"

Megan is adept at instigating adaptive action, which in this case led to tremendous opportunities within an entirely new paradigm. For many leaders, however, fear is a powerful emotion that interferes with their ability to think, make good decisions, and take adaptive action. Everyone feels fear, anger, jealousy, attachment, and other unhelpful emotions once in a while, but when these powerful emotions cause you to think small, become manipulative, use others without giving back, and reduce the infinite possibilities of life, they rob you of resilience.

Daniel Goleman (2004) recounts a strategy for dealing with destructive emotions that Buddhist monk and author Matthieu Ricard refers to as "staring back." Ricard explains that when thoughts associated with fear and other destructive emotions begin, they usually spawn another thought and then another, until "our mental landscape becomes invaded by thoughts that solidify our anger or jealousy—and then it's too late. Just as when a spark of fire has set a whole forest on fire, we are in trouble" (p. 214). Leaders that learn to recognize resilience-inhibiting emotions and thoughts when they arise can also learn to interrupt their proliferation. Ricard says that staring back means that we first register the fact that we are in the grip of a powerful emotion, but we then stare it down with objectivity and reason.

Remember, You Have Skills

One of the easiest ways to get a grip on yourself in the presence of fear is to remember that you have skills. If you haven't seen the movie *Napoleon Dynamite*, put it on your list of things to do this coming weekend. In the film (no spoiler alert here), you'll see the main character, Napoleon, and his buddy, Pedro—two awkward and alienated high schoolers—achieve unthinkable goals by reminding themselves they have skills and then using them in intrepid pursuit of their goals. They even lend their skills to each other and they cajole each other to "get some skills."

Nurse leader Lisa McDonald believes that nurses who intentionally seek opportunities to learn new skills and information and combine them with their internal passion, reach a point in their career where they know they can make a difference. Lisa says,

You have to have passion and you have to be at a place in your career where you know you can take action." She adds, "I am confident of myself, as a person with good thinking skills and my ability to present my ideas verbally.

During times of unexpected change, even highly skilled, talented, and wise leaders can succumb to self-doubt. While it may be a strength to be aware of what you don't currently know, believing that you lack what you need to rise to the challenges before you is not. Remember, you did not get this far in your career without learning a thing or two about how the world works! Even though every new situation is different, do not be bullied by fear of the unknown. You have skills.

Defining Moments and Wise Decisions

Eventually, adaptive action creates information that leads to decisions. Decision-making in complex organizations is difficult enough when things are going well. During disruptive change—when, by definition, the environment is unstable and the way forward is unclear—decision-making is even more of a challenge.

For leaders, the stakes are high. Decisions made during times of disruptive change are defining moments; not only do they mark turning points for the organization, but they also crystallize the abilities of the leader for good or ill in the minds of stakeholders. Wise decisions during times of crisis and change become part of the leader's legacy. Unwise decisions can destroy reputations. For example, one nurse manager, "Patricia" told me (Elle) she regretted not listening to her gut about a colleague, "Joe," who had the habit of making sexist comments to her and telling her raunchy jokes. At the time, Patricia's organization was losing nurses to a higher paying hospital in the area in record numbers. Additionally, the underground opinion was that nurses were fleeing not to earn more money, but to escape an oppressive management team. Patricia wanted to get along with Joe, and even though some of things he said bothered her, she didn't want to be known as "that leader who takes everything so seriously and who everyone is afraid to be themselves around." Thus, Patricia never gave Joe feedback, and never addressed the sexual harassment protocols.

When a patient with a known drug addiction reported Joe for the same offense, Patricia still did not take action. Because of the patient's shaky reputation, she did not follow protocol. A month later when a rash of patients reported Joe and went above Patricia's head to do so, Patricia found herself in as much hot water as Joe was. "In retrospect, it was a mistake to overlook Joe's behavior. If only I followed my gut, I would have been a better leader."

Under ordinary conditions, nurse leaders are expected to support strategic decisions through evidence-based decision-making. When leaders make decisions during disruptive change, however, data about what works in the new reality sometimes does not exist or exists in non-rational forms or locations outside of where the disruption originated. In place of hard data, resilient leaders do not despair. They draw on information wherever they can, both within and outside of the organization (Kaplan, 2012), including what they learn from trying things out, from the counsel of trusted people in their network, from wisdom within the field at large, and from their own intuition. For example, Ebbin Howard was a relatively new nurse leader in 1999, when organizational leaders were absolutely convinced that technology would fail catastrophically at we entered the year 2000 and the 21st century. Ebben says,

> *Everyone was worried about what was going to happen so I said, 'Let's just shut the system down ourselves now and see what happens—lets treat it like we do a hazmat drill.' Of course everyone was freaked out about it, but it worked out just fine. Sometimes we are most creative about problem solving when our back is up against the wall.*

As was described in the previous chapter, Want Something More, the enduring elements of the organizational vision helps leaders make good decisions. Where vision leaves off however, gut feelings and intuition fill in. Especially when the system is in commotion, leaders who do not listen to their gut feelings (or lessons from other areas in their life) miss out on a powerful source of information.

In the irreverent but uncanny distillation of enduring wisdom on the pratfalls of national defense, the brilliant Norman Augustine (1983) writes "Ninety percent of the time things will turn out worse than you expect. The other ten percent of the time you had no right to expect so much" (p. 19). No matter what decisions a leader makes during times of disruptive change, they could be wrong. The corollary to this rule seems to be this: The higher the stakes and turbulence in the environment, the less perfect the decision. Bottom line, in every change there are both dangers and opportunities. Resilience is seen in leaders who focus on the opportunities and leverage them in spite of the risk.

Igniting a Culture of Inquiry

Ohio State University Dean Bern Melnyk asks "What if every nurse walked into work each day asking themselves, 'Is what I'm doing based on evidence?'" Inquiry has a way of sustaining passion—as you investigate the best of what the profession offers, you are highly engaged in understanding your practice. As Melnyk says, "Inquiry keeps the purpose of nursing alive."

According to Dean Melnyk, nurse leaders are key to creating cultures where adaptive action and innovation thrive. "Step zero," she says, "is building the culture by where you are constantly learning and growing. You've got to create an infrastructure for evidence-based practice (EBP)." Dean Melnyk offers several ideas for building an EBP infrastructure including:

1. Get an expectation of EBP into the mission and the vision of the organization
2. Establish a mentor program for EBP
3. Nurture a group of champions interested in leading EBP
4. Build in a system of recognition and support for nurses who engage in EBP

Interestingly enough, a national survey conducted by Melnyk and her colleagues (Melnyk, Gallagher-Ford, Long, Fineout-Overholt, 2014), revealed that although CNOs put quality and safety at the top of their list of priorities, they place EBP at the bottom of the list. "This is a disconnect in thinking," says Dean Melnyk. "They don't see that EBP is a strategy for achieving quality and safety."

The disconnect Dean Melnyk describes is perpetuated at least in part by an emphasis in universities on producing rigorous research without a similar emphasis on how practitioners can translate and apply the research in their practice. The second part of the equation, applying the research, is EBP in action. Melnyk says, "The people who are practicing should be able to use the best evidence available to make the practice better. We need to do better at translating research into practice at a faster rate."

Nurse leader Rachelle Larsen has observed a shift in perspective in recent years, particularly among new nurses, who, more and more often, come from university systems that indoctrinate student nurses in the ideals of EBP. Rachelle says, "We help students identify a problem; something a patient or staff is dealing with. Then, they frame the question, do the research into the problem and create an intervention. Then, they present their findings to the faculty." Rachelle went on to say:

> *What I find is that these new and often young nurses are starting to expect to work in organizations that support this way of thinking. They are more likely to questions practices that do not seem right or that they can find a better way of doing.*

Cultures of EBP do so much more than create research; they instill the practice of translating research deep into the culture. As Dean Melnyk says, "Vision plus execution leads to the best outcomes for patients."

Summary

Resilient leaders recognize that adversity brings opportunities—not the least of which is the innovation that arises from taking adaptive action. Adaptive action assumes that organizational learning is the goal, not perfection. Leaders who are reluctant to take action must deal with the fears that undermine their confidence. Once action is underway, leaders and their colleagues can begin to hone and refine the emerging innovations. In healthcare organizations, evidence-based practice instills quality and innovation deep in the culture. Ultimately, what leaders learn from taking adaptive action allows them to make better decisions that help the organization bounce forward.

Activities and Questions

1. With a particular challenge from your leadership work in mind, and as you reflect on the content in this chapter, what will you draw from the leadership resilience-enabling capacities of Relationships, Resonance, and Renewal, and how do you need to bolster them?

   The leadership challenge I'm thinking of is:

2. In order to help myself and others Instigate Adaptive Action, I need to draw on these ideas from the three leadership resilience enablers:

   • Relationships:

   • Resonance:

   • Renewal:

3. What stories do you have about taking adaptive action in your life or work that you can share with others?

   What was the experiment?

   What did you revise, throw out, and keep?

   What were the key insights about taking adaptive action that you still think of today?

4. Does your culture support adaptive innovation?

   How do people in your organization feel about experiments and experiences on a small scale—where the outcome is uncertain but where the potential for learning about what works is high?

   How would you introduce the concept of adaptive action to your leaders or your unit, department, clinic, or organization?

5. What structures in your organization support or diminish the practice of adaptive innovation? For you? For others?

6. What are you aware of when you make decisions based on a large amount of intuition?

   What happens when you ignore your intuition? Tell your team about a time when either you ignored or listened to your intuition when making a decision.

7. What adaptive action is underway now in your organization?

   Who is trying out a strategy or initiative with the passionate intention to produce valuable results?

   Help the leaders of that experiment document their revisions for the next wave of participants. Take photos, record testimonials, gather and tell early impact people stories, and support them in making presentations and presenting their results.

11

Reflect, Celebrate, and Renew

The hardness of life I deplore creates the qualities I admire.

—Florida Maxwell-Scott, 1968

> *Reminder:* As you read this chapter, note where the ideas and strategies presented draw on the leadership resilience-enabling capacities of relationships, resonance, and renewal. Then, at the end of the chapter, write down what you want to learn about or experience in order to bolster your capacities so that you are better able to respond in the aftermath of adversity and disruptive change.

Now we have reached the point in the cycle of leadership resilience in action when you take a step back and reflect on how the journey is progressing. In this phase, leaders ask questions including: What have we gained? What strategies are taking us into the next turn? What have been the best lessons learned? What needs to be commemorated and celebrated? How are we better because of this experience? What lessons transfer to other challenges? How will the organization change?

Reflection and celebration make great companions to transformational change. Through reflection, we become more aware about what and how we think, feel, and know about ourselves, others, and the world around us. Celebration of course is the way to commemorate, honor, and admire not just what has gone well, but what we learn and how we change from what hasn't gone well as we leveraged adversity into growth.

Personal Reflection and Celebration

Through critical reflection, resilience transforms into wisdom. In the aftermath of disruptive change, resilient leaders make countless passes through the process of reflection and celebration even while uncertainty and ambiguous conditions prevail. This is what the late Donald Schon (1983) describes when he bids professionals to move from technical rationality, where every problem has an answer, to "reflection in action," where professionals respond more intuitively to changing conditions with "artful competence" (p. 19). Of the many insights Schon provided to the fields of professional development and organizational learning, the idea that we can all reflect on what we are doing while we are doing it is profound. Schon, who was himself a jazz musician, compared reflection in action and reflection on action to playing in a jazz group improvising in response to the music. Schon says these musicians are "reflecting-in-action on the music they are collectively making and on their individual contributions to it, thinking what they are doing and, in the process evolving their way of doing it" (p. 56).

Meta Resilience

When you reflect on your resilience, you become even more resilient. Reflection in action takes you beyond thinking about what happened and what you did about it. It also finds you thinking about why you responded the way you did with each action. It gets you to fine tune actions according to the response they elicit from others and the surrounding environment. Thinking about your resilience while you are responding to adversity with resilience requires mindfulness about doing so. But this mindfulness also creates great freedom; your responses are improvisational and relevant in the moment. Leaders who are undisciplined in reflective thinking, on the other hand, tend to perceive only what they expect, through preexisting paradigms. This limits their freedom and their creativity.

Anne Naidoo, a nurse leader in Saudi Arabia, makes a strong case for thinking about what you think and believe about your resilience. Naidoo observes, "Nurses lose and gain every day; it is like living next to a train track—you just get used to responding. We have to learn to refocus from time to time." According to Peter Senge (1990), reflective leaders like Naidoo elevate their mastery of resilience. Senge says:

> *What distinguishes people with high levels of personal mastery is that they have developed a higher level of rapport between their normal awareness and their subconscious. What most of us take for granted and exploit haphazardly, they approach as a discipline.* (p. 162)

Consider the story of Jesse, a successful nurse educator working in a prestigious university. Reflecting back on her late teens and early twenties when her headstrong nature told her to do exactly the opposite of whatever an authority figure told her to do, Jesse recalls being completely aware that she was making choices that were not always in her best interest. Back then, however, she did not know how to pull herself out of the strong emotions of anger, resentment, and powerlessness, and often found herself involved in painful situations. She recalls thinking *What am I doing? What am I doing? I am messing up what could be my life!* This repeated sequence in Jesse's youthful years created a strong emotional memory that serves her well today. When she feels those same emotions coming over her, she knows what they mean—and she now has the ability and wisdom to interrupt her habitual response and mindfully choose to respond more resonantly.

Jesse's reflective nature is different from many leaders who are trapped within what Chris Argyris (in Senge, 1990) says are "defensive routines" that protect them from becoming aware of where they need to change and grow. Reflective leaders like Jesse have learned that powerful emotions draw their attention to opportunities for reflection. These leaders look around them and ask themselves, *What am I doing here? Am I reacting in ways that makes the situation better or worse?*

Pathways to Personal and Organizational Reflection and Celebration

While the reflective strategies resilient leaders choose will differ, all highly resilient leaders are also highly reflective. In this section you'll find a few powerful approaches to increase reflection. Experiment with them to discover what works for you. Keep in mind that one way to know if a reflective strategy is working for you is to notice if it empowers you to improvise and respond in ways that help you and your organization bounce forward.

Have a Thought Leadership Partner

A powerful way to make reflection a practice is to team up with a thought leadership partner (Allison et al., 2012; Allison-Napolitano, 2013). Thought leadership partners are colleagues and coaches who think alongside of you, putting the best knowledge in the field on the table for you to look at and chew over. Thought leadership partners help us reflect by asking open-ended questions and bringing up theories, much more often than they give advice or share their own opinions. They introduce perspectives that are different from yours and that have the ability to jar your mind and challenge your cognitive distortions. Thought leadership partners also just listen.

For many nurse leaders, reflecting with a thought partner is different from reflecting alone. As one leader puts it,

> *When I can process and plan aloud, like I can in coaching sessions, I think about things in a different way. Alone I think about what I have to do. With a thought partner I also think about what I am learning.*

Another leader says:

> *I've had situations where I just need help in thinking something through. When I can't see past my blind spots, I talk with people who will ask me the right questions and give me another perspective. This happened recently*

when I had my mind made up about how to handle an employee grievance. Then, someone introduced a new way of thinking about it and I ended up totally changing my mind.

Showcase Small and Early Wins

Not only does focused action create momentum toward positive change in response to loss and challenges, but it also garners early wins, which inspire confidence in supporters and doubters alike (Watkins, 2003). Leaders who celebrate and broadcast early wins and small wins activate another approach to reflection not only for themselves, but for the entire organization. Any progress toward what you want more of, any movement toward achieving milestones, is worth noticing. As a nurse administrator from a mid-west school of nursing told me, "Our goal is to double the school's enrollment over the next ten years. In the first two years we increased enrollment by 80 students. That might not sound like a lot, but eighty is more than zero!" When leaders celebrate and broadcast small and early wins, the effect goes beyond praising people and programs to inform and refine the next steps. This is an example of true reflection-in-action.

Small wins are changes in the right direction of anything you want more of: more student nurses enrolled, more staff nurses using new skills, more patients satisfied, more patients infection free, and more patients achieving wellness on multiple indicators. For example, one nurse leader wanted student nurses in the mentor program to be more engaged in patient care by asking thoughtful questions either before or after rounds. For one week, she asked the students to give themselves a hash mark in their notebooks every time they asked a question. At the end of the week, she and the mentors met with the student nurses and they celebrated the number of questions asked and also took time to discuss the issues the questions raised.

Increasing the number of questions asked by student nurses may be a small win when it comes to increasing student engagement, but it is a small win in the right direction and on something that matters. One of the most important steps in celebrating small wins is in knowing where they actually exist in the data and then setting up efficient systems to monitor their progress.

With a relentless focus on leveraging disruptive change to motivate toward the vision of the organization, small wins do not mean small goals. Harvard Business School researchers Teresa Amabile and Steven Kramer found that when it comes to change, small wins being recognized regularly confirms for people that they are making progress on meaningful work (2011).

Keep a Journal of Your Favorite Mistakes

With just a few moments of painful reflection, most of us can come up with several examples in our personal and professional lives when we really blew it. Perhaps we missed an opportunity, stayed in a bad relationship far too long, put our faith in someone who turned out to be unreliable, or we failed to follow through on a commitment. Although these blunders and poor calls make you wince when you think of them, most likely they also rendered powerful lessons that changed you and made you a little wiser. Favorite mistakes are those missteps where we learn the most.

One way to wring the maximum amount of learning out of your favorite mistakes is to keep a journal that lingers not on what actually went wrong, but on what you learned about yourself and about the system when it went wrong. The favorite mistakes journal is a tool that often leads to deep learning about how the organization actually prevents its own success. This type of learning is what Donald Schon and Chris Argyris, among others, refer to as double-loop learning. Double-loop learning means that, instead of just learning what doesn't work and trying something different, when you learn that something doesn't work, you look deeper into structures in the system to learn how they help or hinder the situation. In double-loop learning, the remedies go beyond the surface from simply solving one problem to reengineering the underlying contributors to problems.

By its nature, nursing is one of those professions where the stakes are high both for the lives of patients and for a nurse's career. The idea that mistakes could be beneficial is a bit anxiety-producing. Richard Billingsley, a CNO in a southern rural healthcare system says,

> As direct care front-line nurses, we were told not to make any mistakes. Now, as nurse leaders we are expected to be innovative. Even though I know mistakes are how you learn, a big part of me still says, 'I don't want to make a mistake!' As nurses, we don't fail very well!

Leaders who reflect on and celebrate favorite mistakes do more than increase organizational learning: They also steer the culture toward accepting the idea that mistakes produce the most profound learning and ought to be mined for the pearls of wisdom they contain. Nurse leader Lisa Price from Oakland, California, says:

Being transparent with my staff helps me; I don't have to carry the burden of failing quietly, silently in an isolating way. But what is really exciting is the sentiment of transparency is being translated into the culture. Before a meeting, I let the nurses know we'll be talking about something that didn't go well for one of them, as an anonymous case study. Usually, when I'm in the middle of the case study, the nurse involved will just speak up and talk about what they learned. At first I was nervous about this—I didn't want them to be embarrassed and so I tried to protect them with anonymity. But then I decided to relax and let them have their moment—let them say, 'yeah I screwed up but this is what I learned.' Now I celebrate the fact that I've modeled something that people find valuable, and helps them increase their level of practice.

Hold a Learning Fair

In his book *Leading in a Culture of Change* (2001), Michael Fullan says, "If you remember one thing about information, it is that it only becomes valuable in a social context" (p. 78). Building on this idea, Fullan suggests holding a "learning fair," which provides a powerful social context for knowledge building and is an "opportunity to showcase, reflect and celebrate" (p. 101).

Knowledge building strategies such as the learning fair not only encourages reflection, but it also builds relationships. Fullan quotes Nancy Dixon from her book *Common Knowledge*, which states, "If people begin sharing ideas about issues they see as really important, the sharing itself creates a learning culture" (in Fullan, 2001, p. 84).

Celebrate Good Practice

When it comes to leveraging strengths and opportunities, resilient leaders never miss a chance to celebrate. Most leaders celebrate marked improvements in patient outcomes, but leaders that want to increase their resilience and the resilience of others do not wait to accomplish goals before they commemorate positive changes toward those goals. In addition, these leaders do not limit themselves to celebrating changes in outcomes; they also mark positive changes in organizational learning.

Organizational learning, a concept and term coined by Peter Senge in 1990, is seen when—through experience, collaboration, and reflection—individuals and teams contribute new insights to the organization that ultimately and fundamentally refine and reshape it. Savvy leaders pay attention to the process of organizational learning by celebrating changes in people and the culture that signify movement toward powerful practices.

For example, when nurse leader Connie Hill was director of a unit at Children's Memorial Hospital in Chicago, and they received an award that came with some cash, she arranged for several different off-hour team building events for her nurses. The events were chosen based on what the nurses said they loved to do including a champagne night at a local museum, salsa dancing, jewelry making, and a picnic afternoon at a pumpkin patch. But Connie, who knew these playful interludes could also provoke creative problem solving, added one extra requirement. She asked the nurses to come back from their celebration event with novel ideas for improving certain initiatives on the floor. Connie says, "Making the experience work-related allowed people to stretch as a staff—especially for those who were not always active in other social events. They came back with great ideas and an expanded view of themselves as a creative team."

Celebration reinforces good practice. Leaders like Connie Hill know that frequent and specific feedback about behaviors that pave the road to success is also a strategy for resilience.

Reflect-in-Action

I (Elle) am a prolific recorder of memos to myself on my iPhone. The messages I send to myself contain my reflections and insights as they occur to me, usually when I am running or hiking (I've sent myself hundreds of endorphin-catalyzed messages over the years) but also while I work and interact with clients. As a method for reflection in action, your smartphone is an invaluable tool. For example, the novice nurse leader named Lee, whom you met in Chapter 8, is now using his smartphone to record a brief sentence or two about what he is thinking each time he either expresses a negative and skewed perspective or when he successfully recognized he was about to say something rash and unhelpful but stopped himself from doing so. Lee shares these recordings with his leadership coach, who helps him think out loud about what it means, what he can learn about himself, where he needs to make apologies, and what he needs to do in order to behave better the next time.

You can also use your smartphone to record a sentence or two that gives a colleague feedback about something they handled well or performed with artistry. Make the recording, and then simply email it to the other person. Your feedback will mean a lot to them and will go far to bolster their resilience for the day.

Summary

The cycle of leadership is incomplete without reflection and celebration. Reflection and celebration transform the lessons that come from leadership resilience into wisdom—for you, for the people you lead, and ultimately for the entire organization and profession. Keeping in line with what Florida Maxwell-Scott wrote in 1968 when she was well into her eighties—"The hardness of life I deplore creates the qualities I admire"—some of the best lessons come from what does not go well while you respond to adversity (2013, p. 47).

Activities and Questions

1. With a particular challenge from your leadership work in mind, and as you reflect on the content in this chapter, what will you draw from the leadership resilience-enabling capacities of Relationships, Resonance, and Renewal, and how do you need to bolster them?

   The leadership challenge I'm thinking of is:

2. In order to help myself and others Reflect, Celebrate, and Renew I need to draw on these ideas from the three leadership resilience enablers:

   • Relationships:

   • Resonance:

   • Renewal:

3. Try out one or more of the reflection-in-action strategies presented in this chapter, and share your reflections about how they worked for you with a leadership coach, colleague, or your team.

4. As a team, divide up the reflection-in-action strategies presented in this chapter and commit to using the one assigned to you each day for two weeks. Then, come back again as a team and teach the strategy assigned to you to your colleagues. Share what you learned about the strategy as well as yourself, and make suggestions for applying it further in your organization.

IV

Synthesizing the New Resilience

Assessing Your Organization's Level of Risk for Non-Resilience

Even the best leaders cannot predict a specific disruptive change, adverse incident, or wild card event. What leaders can do, however, is influence organizational resilience—an organization capable of bouncing forward from unpredictable events, disruptive change, or adverse incidents. This means that if you want to lead in an environment that supports, values, and enhances your leadership resilience and the resilience of others, you need to intentionally design and mindfully sustain a resilient organization.

This chapter answers these questions:

- What are key risk factors that signal organizational fragility?
- How can you engage other leaders and stakeholders in conversations that help them embrace the reality that adversity is neither unusual nor rare and is essential to growth, positive developmental change, and sustainability?
- What are the leadership actions you must take to build a culture that inspires and sustains resilience?

Developing a Resilient Organizational Culture

Resilient leaders and organizations accept the idea that adversity is neither rare nor unusual. Resilient leaders make resilience a personal and corporate value. They mindfully nurture and sustain its defining qualities and appreciate resilient risks and benefits.

Figure Out If Something Is Fragile

In his book *Antifragile: Things That Gain From Disorder* (2012), Nassim Taleb applies ideas about the fragility and antifragility of financial markets to other complex systems. Taleb provocatively suggests that stability is like a time bomb—one that conceals vulnerabilities that ultimately makes a system fragile. Invoking the metaphor of a forest fire to explain this idea, Taleb writes that "the absence of fire lets highly flammable materials accumulate" (p. 105). Taleb's implication is clear: The inevitable fire will be, at least initially, devastating.

Inviting disorder may sound like a crazy thing to do, but since adversity is neither rare nor unusual—and usually leads to insight and creativity—leaders who purposefully introduce disorder learn where vulnerabilities exist and how to strengthen the system. As Taleb advises, "It is far easier to figure out if something is fragile than to predict the occurrence of an event that may harm it" (Taleb, 2012, p. 4).

Conversations to Introduce Disorder

Resilient leaders don't wait for ticking time bombs to explode on their own; they purposefully set them off. How? During times of apparent stability, they use the art of conversation and discourse to routinely scrutinize their organizations for vulnerabilities. These conversations invite disorder and discovery. Disruptive conversations are often uncomfortable—especially for those who subscribe to the "if it ain't broke, don't fix it" philosophy. Leaders cannot predict or stave off adverse situations, however, they can help leaders and their organizations anticipate adversity and respond with insight and innovation.

Authors of the book *The Innovator's DNA: Mastering the Five Skills of Disruptive Innovators* say that leaders become comfortable in the role of disruptive innovator by asking status-quo-challenging questions that explore key initiatives and uncover vulnerabilities in the way things are being done (Dyer et al., 2011). Asking status-quo-challenging questions is risky because they threaten those who are comfortable with the current state, but resilient organizations sustain themselves only by being willing to change.

A Tool to Introduce Innovative Disruption

The Resilience Risk Assessment is a tool for starting conversations that promote dialogue and discovery. Revealing risks enables stakeholders to take stock of key harbingers of non-resilience. There are at least eight conditions— time bombs if you will—that alert people to potential cracks in the resilience of an organization. In this final section of the book, you'll have the opportunity to learn about the risks and kick off conversations in your organization that lead to discovery, insight and action. First use the assessment to alert you to the current level of risk in your organization. Then, devise a plan of action to make your organization antifragile by moving it from its current state of resilience toward the exemplar.

The eight risks to organizational resilience that we'll examine here are:

1. Top leaders have stopped learning.
2. We blame everything on the budget.
3. We ignore results on critical indicators.
4. We have too many unfocused initiatives, so now people say they have too much on their plate.
5. Success is uncelebrated.
6. We neglect our responsibility to develop leaders within our organization.
7. Our culture stifles nurse innovations.
8. Our work environment is detrimental to the health and well-being of people.

The Resilience Risk Assessment

For each risk, use the exemplar provided to assess your organization's level of risk. The more your organization resembles the exemplar, the less you are at risk for non-resilience. The less your organization resembles the exemplar, the more you are at risk for non-resilience. You can assess your organization's risk level using this six-step process:

Step 1. For each of the eight Resilience Risks, first read the summary that introduces the risk.

Step 2. After you read the summary, read through the bulleted exemplars, which describe the risk at its least vulnerable and most desirable state. The exemplars flesh out an aspirational level of resilience for the risk. This is the level that organizations should aspire to achieve.

Step 3. After you read through the exemplars, rate your organization from 1–10 with 10 representing a direct match with the exemplar and with 1 representing the exact opposite of the exemplar.

Step 4. Compare your rating with other members of your team or organization and talk about the areas where the organization is vulnerable.

Step 5. Use the Thought Leadership Questions to stimulate additional conversation within your leadership team and others.

Step 6. Decide what action you will take in order to move closer to the exemplars for each risk.

Resilience Risk 1: Top Leaders Have Stopped Learning

Summary: Learning is just another word for change and as Peter Senge (1990) wrote, "Organizations learn only through individuals who learn" (p. 139). When things are going well, change is the last thing some leaders want to do, and so they skimp on learning. Especially when budgets are tight, professional development is often the first thing to go.

When top leaders in the organization quit learning, it means they believe they know everything they need to know. This is a form of hubris. Of course, organizations are dynamic; they are in a constant state of change and leaders must continually learn about these changes. When top leaders in the organization quit learning, they put their resilience and the resilience of the organization at risk.

The Exemplar for "Not at Risk"

- We have a yearly learning agenda for each of the top initiatives in our organization. Our learning agenda includes opportunities to learn skills and processes for each initiative, and it includes learning experiences to build our understanding of systems, people, and theories of change.

- We engage in weekly events to learn about our top initiatives. Learning may involve analyzing performance data, attending professional development and training (on one's own and with others), attending book and article studies, holding focus groups with stakeholders, shareholders, employees, suppliers, clients, or customers.

- We speak with front-line employees and stakeholders/patients/families every single day to gain their perspective about how our top initiatives are working.

- We have identified key individuals to coach and mentor into leadership roles for the top initiatives of the organization. These individuals engage in a minimum of twice-monthly coaching/mentoring sessions.

- We identify one reflective question to illuminate each month, and we use it to analyze one or more of our top initiatives. These questions focus our inquiry and provide a framework for the insights we share with each other during our weekly learning agenda meetings.

- We have a leadership feedback and evaluation system that links to aspirational nurse leadership standards and we provide support to help leaders become better.
- Our leaders set an example of lifelong learning and they are transparent about their own need to learn. On the job, they ask other people to teach them.

How vulnerable is your organization for this resilience risk?

Top Leaders in the organization have stopped learning.

Your rating:

In serious risk				*In moderate risk*				*Not at risk*	
1	*2*	*3*	*4*	*5*	*6*	*7*	*8*	*9*	*10*

Resilience Risk 2: We Blame Everything on the Budget

Summary: Like time, money is finite. Every enterprise has a budget to match its mission, scope, and scale. Some organizations—especially those that use government funds and depend on local and state taxes and grants—make poor decisions when cash flow is strong. Often, when funding is cut, programs to assist the most vulnerable populations are the first to go. In addition, some organizations don't monitor the value added by important initiatives and therefore do not make revisions that keep them relevant and non-negotiable when hard times fall.

During times of economic fluctuation, non-resilient leaders place margin over mission; they make cuts across the board without regard for the mission and values of the organization. Or they fail to challenge decisions to keep programs that no longer make sense. These individuals present themselves as victims of the economy and other forces out of their control. Their complaints focus on scarcity and signal a lack of resilience. They cut corners in important initiatives, which creates vulnerabilities in the system that will surface and undermine success when better economic times prevail. These leaders create anxiety and stifle innovation throughout the organization.

The Exemplar for "Not at Risk"

- Anyone can look at our budget and immediately tell what our priorities are.

- We add value to the organization by providing care that over time produces the best outcomes at the lowest cost.

- When we talk about the budget between ourselves and with the larger group of stakeholders, shareholders, employees, the board, and patients and community members, we talk as much about our values and mission as we do cash flow and payments due. Whether the economy is good or bad our budget always reflects our best work.

- In the face of economic pressure, we strive to operate in a culture of care.

- We support innovative ideas that we evaluate for impact and for consistency with our mission and values. Innovation does not mean we lose focus or pursue every new idea. In fact, often our innovations are incarnations and extensions of our best current approaches, and this maintains their relevancy in a changing world. These innovations ultimately strengthen our budget; they attract additional revenue.

- We sustain our best existing initiatives with support systems (e.g. professional development, coaching, talented workforce, leadership) that keep them vibrant and cutting edge. We know this is especially important during tough economic times. After all, why would we neglect our best and most focused work and then have to do double duty to restore and recover them?

How vulnerable is your organization for this resilience risk?

We blame everything on the budget.

Your rating:

In serious risk				*In moderate risk*				*Not at risk*	
1	2	3	4	5	6	7	8	9	10

Resilience Risk 3: We Ignore Results on Critical Indicators

Summary: Leaders need to know how each and every initiative in the enterprise is performing. Key metrics, which provide essential feedback about how the organization is performing, need to be identified at the beginning of each initiative and for each strategy. When organizations objectively look upon data as information about the current reality, updates on critical indicators are not feared but are embraced for what they teach. Discrepancies between the current reality and the vision spur creative tension.

Regular inspection of important metrics provides three benefits: (1) it maintains a sense of urgency and inspiration; (2) it inspires innovative responses and necessary refinements to strategies; and (3) it reveals victories that can be leveraged for greater returns.

The Exemplar for "Not at Risk"

- We know which indicators are used to track the success of each initiative in our organization. These indicators measure the impact of the strategy and their impact on our mission.

- We measure, analyze, discuss, share, and publish outcomes for each initiative, on a regular schedule. Everyone is aware of the system we have in place to engage this process.

- People in all levels of our enterprise are aware of the indicators and the results our initiatives and strategies achieve. These data are used to refine and revise our approaches.

- Our organization looks at trend data. We understand that trends indicate the results we can continue to expect unless something changes. When we like the direction of the trend, we continue to renew and sustain the initiatives through innovation and support. When we dislike the direction of the trend, we seek to understand the facts and we take action.

- When measuring patient outcomes and engagement, we disaggregate data by ethnicity, gender, age and we especially look at data on historically vulnerable groups including low income and patients with limited English proficiency.

- We look at data that shows us how valued outcomes have changed over the years.

How vulnerable is your organization for this resilience risk?

We ignore results on critical indicators.

Your rating:

In serious risk				*In moderate risk*				*Not at risk*	
1	2	3	4	5	6	7	8	9	10

Resilience Risk 4: We Have Too Many Unfocused Initiatives, So Now People Say They Have Too Much on Their Plate

Summary: Ask almost any person working in an organization in a western culture how they are doing, and they will answer with the words, "I'm very busy." Often, busyness is the number one excuse people give for not getting to the most important work on their plate. Ironically, trivial time-wasters and fires that need putting out today undermine high-leverage action and therefore actually create the crisis situations of tomorrow. In their *Harvard Business Review* article (April 2010), Bruch and Menges refer to this sense of overload as the "acceleration trap." According to Bruch and Menges, organizations caught in the acceleration trap overload people without giving them a break, multiload the system with too many different activities and continually load the system with new initiatives without unloading old ones.

The subtext behind complaints of being too busy is a sense of powerlessness. Leaders who find themselves and others talking about how busy they are, need to take control of their priorities.

The Exemplar for "Not at Risk"

- We do work that has meaning. Even though we are quite engaged throughout the day, we are energized—not busy.
- We can name all of our high impact initiatives and strategies and we use more time and energy focusing on these initiatives than we do on tasks from a low level to-do list.
- We renew and revise our high impact initiatives. We keep them sharp and relevant. Instead of constantly overloading the system with new initiatives, we concentrate on bringing our best work to full implementation. This is not to say that we are not innovative. This is to say that we continue to innovate within our best initiatives and we remain focused on our mission.
- We build in cycles of renewal for people in order to break the busy trap and to create and sustain energy for the most important work we do.
- We do not talk about how busy we are. Instead, we describe our work and how it makes a difference. We manage requests that other people make of us and therefore do not blame others for how we use our time and energy.
- We have processes for terminating non-essential tasks and for using data in order to understand where our best work needs concentrated attention, management, revision, and innovation.

How vulnerable is your organization for this resilience risk?

We have too many unfocused initiatives, so now people say they have too much on their plate.

Your rating:

In serious risk				*In moderate risk*				*Not at risk*	
1	2	3	4	5	6	7	8	9	10

Resilience Risk 5: Success is Uncelebrated

Summary: Great leaders do not celebrate success in a Pollyanna effort to make everyone feel better. Instead, they celebrate success in order to understand what individuals and the system itself does to create success. During times of strife, it is easy to succumb to negative or emotional force fields that are characterized more by fear than inspiration. What's going right in the organization is overshadowed by what's going wrong. The real loss, when this happens, is the opportunity to learn the lessons that could very possibly provide the breakthrough needed to alter the current challenge.

Exemplar for "Not at Risk"

- We look for small wins (anything that is more of what we want) in multiple places in the system.
- We have multiple venues for broadcasting wins (newsletters, websites, meetings, presentations, in person) and we use them in planned intervals and spontaneously when the wins occur.
- We celebrate wins and success achieved by the various groups of employees and stakeholders in the system.
- We engage in dialogue to illuminate the details about wins by asking questions such as: What was the turning point? What could jeopardize our approaches? What does this now make possible? We use the insights that come from these dialogues to advance our strategies.
- We express gratitude and provide specific, positive feedback to each other and to all employee and stakeholder groups in the system.
- We eagerly share our favorite mistakes which are the best lessons that come from taking risks and taking adaptive action to create positive change.
- Our leaders are aware of the contributions of the people around them and they take time to acknowledge good work and innovation.

How vulnerable is your organization for this resilience risk?

Success is uncelebrated.

Your rating:

In serious risk				*In moderate risk*				*Not at risk*	
1	*2*	*3*	*4*	*5*	*6*	*7*	*8*	*9*	*10*

Resilience Risk 6: We Neglect Our Responsibility to Develop Leaders Within Our Organization

Summary: The Integrated Nurse Leadership Program (INLP) has found that the development of effective nurse leadership is associated with better than expected patient care outcomes and improvements in nurse recruitment and retention (IOM 2010). At the same time, the 2010 IOM report *The Future of Nursing: Leading Change, Advancing Health*, which advocates for nurse leadership from the bedside to the board room, and for nurses who serve as full partners with other health care professionals, states: "Yet, not all nurses begin their career with thoughts of becoming a leader" (p.11). Given the powerful impact that nurse leadership has on patient outcomes and the future of health care, resilient organizations make leadership development a strategic priority.

The Exemplar for "Not at Risk"

- Our culture encourages higher levels of education and training for nurse leaders.
- Our budget preserves financial support and resources for leadership development.
- We engage in data-driven workforce planning that assures we have leaders who will take health care into the future.
- We have a plan for identifying promising leaders and we are transparent about our recruitment and hiring process and the qualities of leadership needed.
- Our leadership development program focuses on authentic contexts where theory comes to life in practice through job shadowing, job sharing, internships, and mentoring programs that pair aspiring leaders with current leaders.
- Senior leaders in our organization believe that developing leadership in others is a priority and they demonstrate a long-term investment in people.
- Our culture favors a transformational leadership style over management of the status quo and short-term gains.
- In our organization we celebrate the value of learning as much as we celebrate the outcomes of our efforts.
- We encourage aspiring and current leaders to take the helm of projects that draw on their passions and that move the goals of the organization forward in authentic contexts.
- Our organization has brought leadership coaching and mentoring to scale. Our leaders have learned leadership coaching and mentoring skills, which they skillfully apply on the job to support aspiring and new leaders and veteran colleagues.

How vulnerable is your organization for this resilience risk?

We neglect our responsibility to develop leaders within our organization.

Your rating:

In serious risk				*In moderate risk*				*Not at risk*	
1	2	3	4	5	6	7	8	9	10

Resilience Risk 7: Our Culture Stifles Nurse Innovations.

Summary: The Triple Aim is a challenge to nursing to increase the healthcare quality for patients, to improve population health, and to reduce healthcare costs (Stiefel and Nolan, 2012). Meeting the challenge of the Triple Aim demands innovation, a spirit of inquiry, and nurse leadership in research and in evidence-based practice. In a rapidly changing and competitive global society, innovation assures relevancy. Resilient organizations support nurses as they adapt current practices and create new practices that previously have not existed, but are now necessary and possible.

The Exemplar for "Not at Risk"

- A spirit of inquiry prevails. Nurse leaders are in the habit of examining existing evidence for current practices, investigating where evidence is lacking, exploring new methods and creating evidence for new practices.

- We evaluate the results of new methods, measure outcomes, and we disseminate findings.

- We think as much about meeting healthcare wellness needs as we do about caring for those who are ill. These two paradigms engender creativity.

- We recognize that innovation comes from collected efforts and therefore teams are cross-functional and horizontal as well as vertical.

- Middle and executive leaders understand and support inquiry as a cultural norm.

- Nurse leaders at all levels in the system have access to senior leaders and to colleagues from medicine and other specialty areas who listen to their ideas and value their input.

- We have partnerships with nurse educators and nurse education programs as well as with other professional groups that support inquiry practices and that lend knowledge, skills, and resources.

- We provide opportunities for nurse leaders to learn and apply research skills and to employ an evidence-based practice hallmarked by a spirit of curiosity and inquiry.

- Creativity is nurtured through safety for risk-taking, less fear of making mistakes, and permission to be inquisitive and explore.

- Nurse innovation is publicly honored, rewarded, and celebrated. We create forums, poster sessions, and learning fairs to showcase innovations led by nurses.

- Our leaders mentor others in evidence-based practice in leadership and in clinical practice.

- We've examined our organization for outdated practices, policies, regulations, and habits that limit innovation, and we have revised or eliminated them.

How vulnerable is your organization for this resilience risk?

Our culture stifles nurse innovations.

Your rating:

In serious risk				*In moderate risk*				*Not at risk*	
1	2	3	4	5	6	7	8	9	10

Resilience Risk 8: Our Work Environment is Detrimental to the Health and Well-being of People

Summary: A 2012 Gallup poll shows that compared to physicians, nurses exercise less, smoke more, and have a higher incidence of diabetes, depression, and high blood pressure. At the same time, many work environments for nurses are stress generators, lacking in opportunities for collaboration, shared decision-making, meaningful relationships, recognition, and influencing decisions.

With a growing body of evidence linking healthy work environments for nurses at the point of care to patient safety and to other organizational outcomes, the American Association of Critical-Care Nurses (AACN) has developed a set of standards for establishing and maintaining a Healthy Work Environment (2005) that promote skilled communication, true collaboration, effective decision-making, appropriate staffing, meaningful recognition, and authentic leadership. Organizations that translate these standards into practice will not only increase nurse engagement and reduce turnover, but will also achieve better outcomes (AACN standards are articulated at AACN.org).

The Exemplar for "Not at Risk"

- Our nurse leaders thoughtfully develop staffing ratios to support point of care nurses in their commitment to patient care.
- Our organization is a safe place to work.
- Nurses have enhanced control over their nursing practice and are involved in decisions that affect them.
- Our nurse leaders assess and develop personal cross-cultural competencies and apply them in their interactions with others.
- Nurse leaders at all levels in the organization have opportunities for teamwork, collaboration, and friendship.
- Nurse leaders follow a process and procedure to respond to and address bullying and lateral violence.

- Seeing that their work makes a difference—recognition, appreciation, and involving people in witnessing outcomes.
- Nurses have opportunities for on the job work-related and non-work-related interludes of renewal.
- Nurse leaders at all levels in the system have learned how to skillfully communicate with peers, colleagues, and direct reports.
- Our nurse leaders have skills to manage real-time conflicts in ways that sustain communication and relationships.

How vulnerable is your organization for this resilience risk?

Our work environment is detrimental to the health and well-being of people.

Your Rating:

In serious risk				*In moderate risk*				*Not at risk*	
1	2	3	4	5	6	7	8	9	10

Thought Leadership Questions
Thought leadership questions for Resilience Risk 1: "Top leaders have stopped learning."

- What have we learned this week from employees on the front-line of our initiatives?
- What five questions will we illuminate about our initiatives this month?
- Who are we mentoring or coaching to provide leadership in important initiatives?
- What is our learning agenda each month? This year? What books will we read? What conferences will we attend? How will we use what we learned?

Thought leadership questions for Resilience Risk 2: "We blame everything on the budget."

- What resources and support do our best initiatives need to succeed?
- What will we lose if we don't support our current initiative?
- What becomes possible if we made our current initiative strong and sustainable?
- If we don't support our current initiatives or any other great ideas now, how will we justify adding them back when our budget is stronger?
- What new initiatives will move our goals forward?
- How does our budget reflect our priorities?

Thought leadership questions for Resilience Risk 3: "We ignore results on critical indicators."

- Are we measuring outcomes that reflect the mission of our organization?
- What trends, even slight, do we see? What is the best we make of these trends? What is the worst we make of these trends?
- What else can the data mean?
- What assumptions does the data challenge?
- Who is impacted by the data? What stakeholder groups? What shareholder groups?

Thought leadership questions for Resilience Risk 4: "We have too many unfocused initiatives, so now people say they have too much on their plate."

- What do people in this organization say is our most important work? What percentage of their energy and time goes into this work?
- What are we not getting to that troubles us most?
- What will be our legacy?
- How do we sustain organizational energy?
- How do we promote a culture of renewal?

Thought leadership questions for Resilience Risk 5: "Success is uncelebrated."

- What examples count as early wins in our top three initiatives?
- How do we assure that everyone in the organization knows our current status relative to our desired status?
- How do we use or misuse successes to encourage or discourage people?
- What do we want more of?
- What is worth celebrating in our organization?

Thought leadership questions for Resilience Risk 6: "We neglect our responsibility to develop leaders within our organization."

- What are we learning? What are we teaching others these days?
- What goals in our organization have to do with developing people?
- What is our organization capacity for leadership coaching and mentoring?

- How open are we about supporting the passions of aspiring and current leaders?
- If our organization was really great at developing leadership in others, what would we gain?

Thought leadership questions for Resilience Risk 7: "Our culture stifles nurse innovations."

- From where in the organization do most innovations arise? Who are we leaving out?
- What is our tolerance for inquiry, experimentation, and risk taking?
- How do we acknowledge nurse innovations? What forums do we provide for nurses to collaborate and share what they learn?
- How do we model the spirit of inquiry?
- How do we mentor nurses for inquiry?

Thought leadership questions for Resilience Risk 8: "Our work environment is detrimental to the health and well-being of people."

- How engaged are we, and others in the work of this organization? Are we and are others contributing ideas and accepting leadership for initiatives?
- What are the opportunities for employees to engage in positive conversations and interactions with others in the work place?
- How does our culture truly empower employees to have a say in what happens and how things are done?
- What do our indicators say about employee engagement? What about longevity of employment and absenteeism? Do employees accept new positions and opportunities within our organization? Do they recommend us to their friends and family?
- How do we encourage and model work/life balance? What system supports have we put in place to assure that work/life balance is more than just an idea, but has become a sustainable value in our culture?

Afterword

Forgive Yourself Every Day

*Finish each day and be done with it. You have done
what you could; some blunders and absurdities have
crept in; forget them as soon as you can. Tomorrow is a
new day; you shall begin it serenely and with too high
a spirit to be encumbered with your old nonsense.*

—Ralph Waldo Emerson

In 2000, I (Elle) began a disciplined study of the nature of wisdom. Due to the theoretical conundrums surrounding wisdom—What is wisdom actually? Can wisdom be measured? Is wisdom common or uncommon?—people within the academic wisdom circles I traffic commonly joke that only a fool would consider studying it. Perhaps this explains why I earnestly pursued the topic, eventually earning a doctorate for my dissertation on the nature of wisdom in nurses.

As a true wisdom geek, I continued to interview wise people, from all walks of life, even after I earned my degree. In 2007, I had the great privilege of interviewing Teresa McCoy, a leader in the Eastern Band of the Cherokee Nation, who was also known for her wisdom. I asked Teresa to tell me about love. She said,

No matter what you love—your nation, your community, the organization you lead, your family, or another person—you must wake up every morning and forgive yourself for whatever is bothering you. This is how you make room for the challenges of the new day.

Teresa's words echo the essential and potent messages of virtually every leader I interviewed while writing this book: You must care deeply and show up every day, inspired and confident that you can and will make a difference. You must tenderly forgive yourself for your blunders and foibles—for your humanness. If you do not, you will continue to hold the fear of failure over your own head; and you will be afraid to take risks, lest you fail again.

Above all other strategies, forgiving yourself everyday frees you to bounce forward and continue your work for a greater good.

Sustaining Your Practice of Leadership Resilience

As with any worthwhile practice, the road to excellence begins with commitment. One highly effective strategy for keeping the commitments you make to yourself to put the ideas in this book into action is to tell at least one person about it and ask for his or her support and feedback. Here are a few additional ideas for sustaining your leadership practice of becoming more resilient:

- Make it part of your leadership development goals. Whether you are a nurse leader at the bedside, a charge nurse, or nurse administrator, you most likely have a success plan that outlines your learning goals each year. Tell the person you report to that you would like to make leadership resilience a focus of your goals. Better yet, ask them to read this book with you and meet to talk about it.

- Secure the services of a leadership coach or mentor and invite them to read the book with you and discuss the ideas within as part of your leadership work.

- Keep a journal where you can reflect on the adversities you face in your leadership work and on how you responded and what you learned.

- Consider inviting trusted colleagues to engage in conversation and learning with you on some of the concepts and ideas presented in this book. Develop a Leadership Resilience Learning Group.

- Connect with others in your professional networks to explore and discuss your experiences and learn from each other. Share insights, reflections and discoveries.

Once you make a commitment to yourself to mindfully focus on leadership resilience, take time to read this book and apply what you learn in your life.

As you place your attention on the capacities and actions that make leadership resilience possible, you will cultivate more of it. Don't despair during those times when you feel less resilient. In fact, the experience of being non-resilient is actually good for you to remember, as you will better recognize what it means to bounce forward. When you forget to take guidance from what you know works, simply come back to it. As a practice, coming back to leadership resilience is always possible and always available.

Be a Good Soul

At some point, even though you are not perfect in your own practice of leadership resilience, be willing to coach and mentor a new leader in their practice of bouncing forward. In these roles, you will simultaneously deepen and strengthen your leadership resilience while providing enormous comfort and support to new or aspiring leaders who no doubt face myriad adversities of their own.

References

(ALL URLs were current as of February 24, 2015.)

Allison, E. (2006). *Wisdom and loss: The role of life loss in the lives of nurses thought to be wise*. Ann Arbor, MI: Proquest Information and Learning Company.

Allison, E. (2012). *Renewal coaching fieldbook: How effective leaders sustain meaningful change*. San Francisco, CA: Jossey-Bass.

Allison-Napolitano, E. (2011a). On the job stress busters. Retrieved from http://wisdomout.com/wp-content/uploads/2012/02/On-the-job-stress-busters2.pdf

Allison-Napolitano, E. (2011b). Stare back at fear: 25 things leaders can do everyday. Retrieved from http://wisdomout.com/stare-back-at-fear-25-things-leaders-can-do-everyday/

Allison-Napolitano, E. (2013). *Flywheel: Transformational leadership coaching for sustainable change*. Thousand Oaks, CA: Corwin.

Allison-Napolitano, E. (2014). *Bounce forward: The extraordinary resilience of leadership*. Thousand Oaks, CA: Corwin.

Amabile, T. M., & Kramer, S. J. (2011). *The progress principal: Using small wins to ignite joy, engagement, and creativity at work*. Cambridge, MA: Harvard Business Review Press.

American Psychological Association (APA). (2002). The road to resilience. Retrieved from http://www.apa.org/helpcenter/road-resilience.aspx. (For additional context, see also http://www.apa.org/monitor/oct02/pp.aspx)

American Nurses Association (ANA). (2013). Leadership institute competency model. Retrieved from http://www.analeadershipinstitute.org/Doc-Vault/About-Us/ANA-Leadership-Institute-Competency-Model-pdf.pdf

American Nurses Association (ANA). (2015). *Code of Ethics for Nurses with interpretive statements*. Silver Spring, MD: Author.

Ariely, D. (2010). *Predictably irrational: The hidden forces that shape our destiny*. New York, NY: Harper Perennial.

Ariely, D. (2010, January) The long term effects of short-term emotions. Online *Harvard Business Review*. Retrieved from: https://hbr.org/2010/01/column-the-long-term-effects-of-short-term-emotions/ar/1?cm_sp=Article-_-Links-_-Download

Augustine, N. R. (1983). *Augustine's laws: Revised and enlarged*. New York, NY: American Institute of Aeronautics and Astronautics.

Baber, A., & Waymon, L. (2007). *Make your contacts count: Networking know-how for business and career success.* New York, NY: AMCOM, American Management Association.

Bass, K., & McGeeney, K. (October 2012). U.S. physicians set good health example. *Gallup News Service.* Retrieved from http://www.gallup.com/poll/157859/physicians-set-good-health-example.aspx

Berwick, D. M., Nolan, T. W., & Whittington, J. (2008). The triple aim: Care, health, and cost. *Health Affairs 27*(3), 759–69.

Blackburn, E. H. (2009). Nobel Lecture: Telomeres and telomerase: The means to the end. Nobelprize.org. Retrieved from http://www.nobelprize.org/nobel_prizes/medicine/laureates/2009/blackburn-lecture.html

Block, J. H., & Block, J. (1980). The role of ego-control and ego-resiliency in the organization of behavior. In W. A. Collins (Ed.), *Development of cognition, affect, and social relations: Minnesota Symposia on Child Psychology* (Vol. 13, pp. 39–101). Hillsdale, NJ: Erlbaum.

Bonanno, G. A. (2009). *The other side of sadness: What the new science of bereavement tells us about life after loss.* New York, NY: Basic Books.

Bonanno, G. A., Galea, S., Bucciareli, A., & Vlahov, D. (2007). What predicts psychological resilience after disaster? The role of demographics, resources, and life stress. *Journal of Consulting and Clinical Psychology 75*(5), 671–682.

Box, George E. P., & Draper, N. R. (1987). *Empirical model-building and response surfaces.* San Francisco, CA: Wiley.

Boyatzis, R. E., & McKee, A. (2005). *Resonant leadership: Renewing yourself and connecting with others through mindfulness, hope, and compassion.* Boston, MA: Harvard Business School Press.

Bridges, W. (1980). *Transitions.* New York, NY: Addison-Wesley.

Brown-Easton, L. (2008). *Powerful designs for professional learning* (2nd ed.).Oxford, OH: National Staff Development Council.

Bruch, H., & Menges, J. I. (2010, April). The acceleration trap. *Harvard Business Review 88*(3), 80–86.

Butler, L. D., Blasey, C. M., Garlan, R. W., McCaslin, S. E., Azarow, J., Chen, X. -H., Spiegel, D. (2005). Posttraumatic growth following the terrorist attacks of September 11, 2001: Cognitive, coping, and trauma symptoms predictors in an Internet convenience sample. *Traumatology, 11*, pg. 247–267.

Byrd, J., & Brown, P. (2003). *The innovation equation: Building creativity and risk taking in your organization.* San Francisco, CA: Jossey-Bass/Pfeiffer.

Cacioppo, J. T., & Patrick, W. (2008). *Loneliness: Human nature and the need for social connection.* Boston, MA: Tantor Media.

Calhoun, L. G., & Tedeschi, R. G. (2006). *The handbook of posttraumatic growth: Research and practice.* Mahwah, NJ: Lawrence Erlbaum Associates.

Caruso, D. R., & Salovey, P. (2004). *The emotionally intelligent manager.* San Francisco, CA: Jossey-Bass.

Clavreul, G. M. (2014). Keep that nurse. Retrieved from http://www. workingnurse.com/articles/Keep-That-Nurse

Clay, R., Knibbs, J., & Joseph, S. (2009). Measurement of posttraumatic growth in young people: A review. *Clinical Child Psychology & Psychiatry 14*(3), 411–422.

Cohen, D., & Prusak, L. (2001*). In good company: How social capital makes organizations work.* Boston, MA: Harvard Business School Press.

Crabtree, S. (2013). Worldwide, 13% of employees are engaged at work. Gallup. Retrieved from http://www.gallup.com/poll/165269/worldwide-employees-engaged-work.aspx

Davidson, R. J. (2012). *The emotional life of your brain: How its unique patterns affect the way you think, feel, and live—and how you can change them.* New York, NY: Hudson Street Press.

Davidson, R., Kabat-Zinn, J., Schumacher, J., Rosenkranz, M., Muller, D., Santorelli, S. F., ... Sheridan, J. F. (2003). Alterations in brain and immune function produced by mindfulness meditation. *Psychosomatic Medicine 65*, 564–570.

de Lange, T., Lundblad, V., & Blackburn, E. (2006). *Telomeres* (2nd ed.). USA: Cold Spring Harbor Laboratory Press.

Dyer, J., Gregersen, H., & Christensen, C. M. (2011). *The innovator's DNA: Mastering the five skills of disruptive innovators* [Kindle version]. Perseus Books Group.

Epel, E. S., Blackburn, E. H., Lin, J., Dhabner, F. S., Adler, N. E., Morrow, J. D., & Cawthorn, R.M. (2004). Accelerated telomere shortening in response to life stress. *Proceedings of the National Academy of Sciences 101*, 17312–17315.

Fritz, C. (2012, May). Coffee breaks don't boost productivity after all. Cambridge, MA: *Harvard Business Review 90*(5), 34–35.

Gallup, Inc. (2013). *State of the American workplace: Employee engagement insights for U.S. business leaders.* Washington DC.: Author.

Gallup News Service. (2010). Nursing leadership from the bedside to the boardroom: Opinion leader perceptions. *Top Line Report.* Retrieved from http://www.rwjf.org/content/dam/web-assets/2010/01/nursing-leadership-from-bedside-to-boardroom

Goldstein, A. N., Greer, S. M., Saletin, J. M., Harvey, A. G., Nitschke, J. B., & Walker, M. P. (2013, June 26). Tired and apprehensive: Anxiety amplifies the impact of sleep loss on aversive brain anticipation. *The Journal of Neuroscience 33*(26), 10607–10615. doi:101523/JNEUROSCI.5578–12.2013

Goleman, D. (1998). *Working with emotional intelligence.* New York, NY: Bantam Books.

Goleman, D. (2004). *Destructive emotions: How can we overcome them? A scientific dialogue with the Dalai Lama.* New York, NY: Bantam Books.

Goleman, D. (2011). *The brain and emotional intelligence: New insights* [Kindle version]. Northampton, MA: More Than Sound.

Goleman, D., Boyatzis, R., & McKee, A. (2004). *Primal leadership: Realizing the power of emotional intelligence.* Boston, MA: Harvard Business School Press.

Grady, V. M., & Grady, J. D. (2012). *The pivot point: Success in organizational change.* New York, NY: Morgan James Publishing.

Hamel, G. (2009). Moonshots for management. *Harvard Business Review, 8*(10), 1–9.

Hansen, R. (2013). *Hardwiring happiness: The new brain science of contentment, calm, and confidence.* New York: Harmony Books.

Harland, L., Harrison, W., Jones, J., & Reiter-Palmon, R. (2005). Leadership behaviors and subordinate resilience. *Journal of Leadership and Organizational Studies* 11, 2–14.

Heifetz, R. (1998). *Leadership without easy answers.* Cambridge, MA: Harvard University Press,

Homer-Dixon, T. (2006). The upside of down: Catastrophe, creativity, and the renewal of civilization. Canada: Random House.

Hudson, F. (1999). *The adult years: Mastering the art of self-renewal.* San Francisco: Jossey-Bass.

Ibarra, H., & Hunter, M. (2007). How leaders create and use networks. *Harvard Business Review 85*(1), 40.

Isaacs, W. (1999). *Dialogue and the art of thinking together: A pioneering approach to communicating in business and life.* New York, NY: Doubleday.

Jetten, J., Haslam, C., Haslam, S. A., & Branscombe, N. R. (2009, September). The social cure. *Scientific American Mind 20,* 26–33.

Johnson, S. (2010). *Where good ideas come from: The natural history of innovation.* New York, NY: Riverhead Books.

Kaplan, S. (2012). *Leapfrogging: Harness the power of surprise for business breakthroughs.* San Francisco, CA: Berrett-Koehler.

Kaufman, S., Elliot, M., & Shmueli, D. (2013). Beyond intractability: Frames, framing and reframing. (Original publication September 2003, updated June 2013 by Heidi Burgess.) Retrieved from http://www.beyondintractability.org/essay/framing/

Kim, D. H. (1991). *Introduction to systems thinking.* Waltham, MA: Pegasus Communications.

Knoke, D. (1999). Organizational networks and corporate social capital. In S. M. Gabbay (Ed.), *Corporate social capital and liability* (pp. 17–42). Boston, MA: Kluwer.

Kobasa, S. C. (1979). Stressful life events, personality, and health—Inquiry into hardiness. *Journal of Personality and Social Psychology 37*, 1–11.

Koltko-Rivera, M. E. (2006). Rediscovering the later version of Maslow's hierarcy of needs: Self-transcendence and opportunities for theory, research, and unification. *Review of General Psychology 10*(4), 302–317.

Lauritzen, C., & Jaegar, M. (1997*). Integrating learning through story: The narrative curriculum*. Albany, NY: Delmar Publishers.

Leider, R., & Shapiro, D., (2002*). Repacking your bags: Lighten your load for the rest of your life*. San Francisco, CA: Berrett-Koehler.

Loehr, J. (2007). *The power of story: Change your story change your destiny in business and in life*, NY: Free Press.

Lynch, J. (2000). *A cry unheard: New insights into the medical consequences of loneliness*. Baltimore, MD: Bancroft Press.

Marsh, J. A., Pane, J. F., & Hamilton, L. S. (2006). *Making sense of data-driven decision making in education: Evidence from recent Rand research*. Santa Monica, CA: Rand.

Maxwell-Scott, F. (2013). *The measure of my days: One woman's vivid, enduring celebration of life and learning*. New York, NY: Penguin Books.

McCarthy, D. and Klein, S. (2010). The triple aim journey: Improving population health and patients' experience of care, while reducing costs. *Commonwealth Fund Publication 1421 48*: 1(2010): 1–11.

McKee, A., Johnston, F., & Massimilian, R. (2006, May/June). Mindfulness, hope and compassion: A leader's road map to renewal. *Ivey Business Journal*. Retrieved from http://iveybusinessjournal.com/topics/leadership/mindfulness-hope-and-compassion-a-leaders-road-map-to-renewal#. UnRuWp0o5D8

Melnyk, B., Gallagher-Ford, L., Long, L., & Fineout-Overholt, E. (2014). The establishment of evidence-based practice competencies for practicing registered nurses and advanced practice nurses in real-world clinical settings: proficiencies to improve healthcare quality, reliability, patient outcomes, and costs. *Worldviews Evidence-Based Nursing 11*(1), 5–15. doi: 10.1111/wvn.12021.

Merchant, N. (2013, January 14). Sitting is the smoking of our generation [Web log post]. *Harvard Business Review* Blog Network. Retrieved from http://blogs.hbr.org/2013/01/sitting-is-the-smoking-of-our-generation

Mezirow, J. (2000). Learning to think as an adult: Core concepts of transformation theory. In Mezirow and Associates (Eds.), *Learning as transformation* (pp. 3–34). San Francisco, CA: Jossey-Bass.

Nahapiet, J., & Ghoshal, S. (1998). Social capital, intellectual capital, and the organizational advantage. *Academy of Management Review 23*, 242.

Nichols, M. (1995). *The lost art of listening: How learning to listen can improve relationships.* NY: The Guilford Press.

O'Brien, J. (2011, April 4). Exercise may prevent impact of stress on telomeres, a measure of cell health. PULSE e-Newsletter. Retrieved from http://www.ucsf.edu/news/2011/04/9652/exercise-may-prevent-impact-stress-telomeres-measure-cell-health

Ozbay, F., Johnson, D., Dimoulas, E., Morgan, C., Charney, D., & Southwick, S. (2007, May). Social support and resilience to stress: From neurobiology to clinical practice. *Psychiatry 4*(5), 35–40.

Paris, L. G., & Terhaar, M. (December 7, 2010). Using Maslow's Pyramid and the National Database of Nursing Quality Indicators™ to attain a healthier work environment. *The Online Journal of Issues in Nursing 16*(1), A1.

Perrin, T. (2008). Towers Perrin Global Workforce Study (2007–2008). Closing the engagement gap: A road map for driving superior business performance. www.towersperrin.com

Pesut, D. J. (1991). The art, science, and techniques of reframing in psychiatric mental health nursing. *Issues in Mental Health Nursing 12*(1), 9–18.

Pesut, D. J. (2001). Healing into the future: Recreating the profession of nursing through inner work. In Norma Chaska (Ed.), *The nursing profession: Tomorrow and beyond* (pp. 853–867). Thousand Oaks, CA: Sage Publishers.

Pesut, D. J. (2007). Leadership: How to achieve success in nursing organizations. In Chad O'Lynn and Russell Tranbarger (Eds.), *Men in nursing: History, challenges and opportunities* (pp. 153–168). NY: Springer Publishing.

Pesut, D. J. (2008). The wisdom of renewal. *American Nurse Today 3*(7), 34–36.

Pesut, D. J. (2012). Transforming inquiry and action in interdisciplinary health professions education: A blueprint for action. *Interdisciplinary Studies Journal 1*(4), 53–632.

Peters, T. (2001). Rule #3: Leadership is confusing as hell. *Fast Company.* Retrieved from http://www.fastcompany.com/magazine/44/march-2001

Pink, D. (2009). *Drive: The surprising truth about what motivates us.* New York, NY: Riverhead Books.

Putnam, R. D. (2000). *Bowling alone: The collapse and revival of American community.* San Francisco, CA: Simon-Schuster.

Rath, T., & Conchie, B. (2008). *Strengths based leadership*. New York, NY: Gallup Press.

Reivich, K., & Shatté, A. (2002). *The resilience factor: Seven essential skills for overcoming life's inevitable obstacles* [Kindle version]. Random House.

Rifkin, R. (2015). Americans rate nurses highest on honesty, ethical standards. *Gallup News Service*. Retrieved from http://www.gallup.com/poll/180260/americans-rate-nurses-highest-honesty-ethical-standards.aspx

Sanders, T. (2002). *Love is the killer app: How to win business and influence friends*. New York, NY: Three Rivers Press.

Sapolsky, R. (2004). *Why zebras don't get ulcers: An updated guide to stress, stress-related diseases, and coping* (3rd ed.). New York, NY: Henry Holt & Co.

Scales, P. C., Benson, P. L., Leffert, N., & Blyth, D. A. (2000). Contribution of developmental assets to the prediction of thriving among adolescents. *Applied Developmental Science* 4(1), 27–46.

Schon, D. A. (1983). *The Reflective Practitioner: How professionals think in action*. London, United Kingdom: Temple Smith.

Seligman, M. (2006). *Learned optimism: How to change your mind and your life* (2nd ed.). New York, NY: Vintage Books.

Seligman, M. (2011a). *Flourish: A visionary new understanding of happiness and well-being*. New York, NY: Free Press.

Seligman, M. (2011b, April). Building resilience. *Harvard Business Review 89*(4), 100–6.

Senge, P. M. (1990). *The fifth discipline: The art and practice of the learning organization*. New York, NY: Doubleday.

Sharot, T. (2012). *The optimist bias: A tour of the irrationally positive brain*. New York: Vintage Books.

Siebert, A. (2005). *The resiliency advantage: Master change, thrive under pressure, and bounce back from setbacks*. San Francisco, CA: Berrett-Koehler.

Sigma Theta Tau International. (2005). The scholarship of reflective practice resource paper. Retrieved from http://www.nursingsociety.org/aboutus/PositionPapers/Documents/resource_reflective.pdf

Singer, T. (2011). *Stress less (for women): Calm your body, slow aging, and rejuvenate the mind in 5 simple steps*. New York, NY: Hudson Street Press.

Smith, W. (2009). *The creative power: Transforming ourselves, our organizations and our world*. New York, NY: Routledge.

Sullivan, E. (2013). *Becoming influential: A guide for nurses* (2nd ed.). Boston, MA: Pearson Education.

Stiefel. M, Nolan K., *A guide to measuring the triple aim: Population health, experience of care, and per capita cost*. Cambridge, Institute for Healthcare Improvement.

Sutton, R. I. (2008, August 13). Are you being a jerk? Again? Bloomberg Businessweek. Retrieved from http://www.businessweek.com/stories/2008-08-13/are-you-being-a-jerk-again

Sy, T., Cote S., & Saavedra, R. (2005). The contagious leader: Impact of the leader's mood on the mood of group members, group affective tone, and group processes. *Journal of Applied Psychology 90(2)*, 295–305

Taleb, N., (2012). *Antifragility: Things that gain from disorder*. New York, NY: Random House.

Tedeschi, R. G., & Calhoun, L. G. (1995). *Trauma and transformation: Growing in the aftermath of suffering*. Thousand Oaks, CA: Sage.

Tedeschi, R. G., & Calhoun, L. G. (2004). *Posttraumatic growth: Conceptual foundation and empirical evidence*. Philadelphia, PA: Lawrence Erlbaum Associates.

Tedlow, R. S. (2010). *Denial: Why business leaders fail to look facts in the face—and what to do about it*. New York, NY: Penguin Group.

Tomajan, K. (January 31, 2012). Advocating for nurses and nursing. *The Online Journal of Issues in Nursing* 17(1), Manuscript 4.

Tombaugh, J. R. (2005). Positive leadership yields performance and profitability: Effective organizations develop their strengths. Development and learning 15-7.

Turner, D. S.; & Cox, H. (2004). Facilitating post-traumatic growth. *Health and Quality of Life Outcomes 2*, 200–216.

Watkins, M. D. (2003). *The first 90 days: Critical success strategies for new leaders at all levels*. Boston, MA: Harvard Business School Publishing.

Wineapple, B. (2009). *White heat: The friendship of Emily Dickinson and Thomas Wentworth Higginson*. New York, NY: Anchor Books.

von Oech, R. (1990). *A whack on the side of the head: How you can be more creative* (revised). New York, NY: Warner Books.

Zautra, A. J., Hall, J. S., & Murray, K. E. (2010). Resilience: A new definition of health for people and communities. In J. W. Reich, A. J. Zautra, & J. S. Hall (Eds.), *Handbook of adult resilience* (pp. 3–34). New York, NY: Guilford.

Zolli, A., & Healy, A. M. (2012). *Resilience* [Kindle version]. New York, NY: Simon & Schuster.

Index